GUIDE TO
BUTTERFLIES
OF BRITAIN AND IRELAND

JEREMY THOMAS

ACKNOWLEDGEMENTS

In preparing the original version of this book, in the early 1980s, I was much helped by Martin Warren, Ken Wilmott, Trevor Dolby and Andrew Branson. I am again indebted to Martin and Ken, and especially to David Simcox and Steve Luck, for help and advice during its transformation into the *Philip's Guide*. Christer Wiklund, Magne Friberg, Maurice Hughes and Brian Nelson provided the new information on Réal's (now called 'Cryptic') and 'other' Wood Whites, and generously allowed me to quote from their unpublished observations. I remain in awe of the skill with which Ken Oliver captured the precise habitats of the young stages in his illustrations of life-cycles, and I am delighted to use Richard Lewington's incomparable illustrations of adult butterflies for the new identification guide. As before, I owe a special debt to many predecessors, notably F. W. Frohawk, Richard South, E. B. Ford, Edmund Sandars, Miriam Rothschild and Margaret Brooks, for the inspiration and knowledge they have imparted. Finally, I was encouraged throughout by Sarah to whom – with our daughters Emily and Anna – this book is dedicated.

First published in 2007 by Philip's,
a division of Octopus Publishing Group Limited
(www.octopusbooks.co.uk)
Endeavour House, 189 Shaftesbury Avenue,
London WC2H 8JY
An Hachette UK Company (www.hachette.co.uk)

Text copyright © 2007, 2014 Jeremy Thomas
Copyright © 2007, 2014 Philip's

Second edition 2014

ISBN 978–1–84907–328–8

A CIP catalogue record for this book is available
from the British Library.

First published as the *RSNC Guide to the
Butterflies of the British Isles*. Subsequently
published as *The Hamlyn Guide to Butterflies
of the British Isles*.

Printed in Thailand

FRONT COVER: *tl* Speckled Wood (*Pararge aegeria*);
tr Large Blue (*Maculinea arion*); *c & br* Small Tortoiseshell
(*Aglais urticae*); *bl* Purple Hairstreak (*Neozephyrus quercus*)
BACK COVER: *left* White Admiral (*Limenitis camilla*)
life-cycle illustration; *right* Purple Hairstreak (*Neozephyrus
quercus*) distribution map
CONTENTS PAGE: *from top* Small Skipper (*Thymelicus
sylvestris*); Brown Hairstreak (*Thecla betulae*); Mountain
Ringlet (*Erebia epiphron*)

Details of other Philip's titles and services
can be found on our website:
www.philips-maps.co.uk

CONTENTS

Introduction	4
The Life-cycle and Structure of a Butterfly	6
Colonies and Numbers	8
Distribution and Habitats	10
Woodland	10
Grassland	14
Butterfly watching in grassland	16
Heaths, moors, bogs and mountains	18
Gardens and hedgerows	20
Garden plants for butterflies	22
Butterfly or Moth?	24
Identification Guide	
How to use the field guide	25
Guide to the main family groups	26
Skippers	28
White butterflies	30
Yellows and Whites	32
Small Copper and Hairstreaks	33
Blues	34
Emperor, Admirals and Vanessids	36
Vanessids	38
Swallowtail	39
Medium-sized and large Fritillaries	40
Large Fritillaries	42
Browns	43
The Butterflies	46–165
Extinct butterflies	166
Rare migrants, vagrants and accidentals	167
Day-flying moths	170
Further Reading and Viewing	173
Societies to Join	174
Index	175

INTRODUCTION

This guide has been written for the growing number of field naturalists who wish to discover and identify the wild butterflies of Britain and Ireland. Wherever possible, I have avoided the use of scientific jargon, in the hope that beginners and children will not be overawed by what is really rather an easy subject to master. On the other hand, I have tried to interest the more expert naturalist by including as much new information as possible about the biology and distribution of our butterflies.

The book has three main sections. The first contains a brief account of the structure and life-cycle of a butterfly, and describes how different species live in different habitats. Next is a 21-page identification guide, with purple-cornered pages for rapid identification, where all except the rarest vagrants are illustrated side by side, with notes on how to distinguish between them. This leads into the main part of the book: a detailed account of the natural history of each species, including illustrations of the whole life-cycle and as much other information as space permits. The young stages have been specially drawn to show how they appear in their natural surroundings; caterpillars and chrysalises are life size, but the eggs are enlarged about seven times.

Every resident species in Britain and all the regular immigrants from abroad are included in the main sections, a total of 60 species. Rare vagrants, that one might encounter once in a lifetime, are relegated to the final pages, alongside a brief description of the extinct Large Copper.

◀ The Large Blue has been successfully reintroduced to Britain following its extinction in 1979. It now breeds on more than 20 carefully managed sites, often in large numbers.

The *Philip's Guide to Butterflies of Britain and Ireland* represents a major revision of my 1986 field guide (The *RSNC*, later the *The Hamlyn Guide*) which, after five impressions, had been unavailable since new publishers inherited the title in 1992. Much has changed in the intervening years, and this is reflected in almost every part of this book. In the species accounts, the 'Habitat and behaviour' sections reflect the burgeoning increase in knowledge resulting from recent research on the ecology of butterflies. Greater changes are found under 'Distribution and status' and in the maps, reflecting not only the calamitous decline of most British butterflies during the past 30 years but also the expansion northwards in range of a sizeable minority of fairly common species that have benefited from the warmer springs and summers. The habitats shown in each illustration of the life-cycle are now presented in colour, providing naturalists with a much better impression of the camouflage or relative conspicuousness of each species' egg, caterpillar and chrysalis in its natural habitat, as well as of the distinctive spots within grasslands, wood or heath where each species may be found. A third of the photographs have been replaced by superior or more characteristic images, and two new species – the re-introduced Large Blue and the newly discovered Cryptic Wood White of Ireland – have been added.

Many naturalists found the identification guide to adult butterflies one of the more useful features of the original book. Here, the format remains unchanged, although it has been expanded slightly and all the illustrations have been replaced by those of Richard Lewington – the leading butterfly illustrator of our time. Not only are the images of superior quality, they now depict the undersides from side-on, more as one sees the butterflies in the wild.

▼ *The Comma has benefited from the warmer climate of the past 30 years and has expanded into cooler parts of Britain more than any other butterfly.*

post 1982 expansion

1982 range

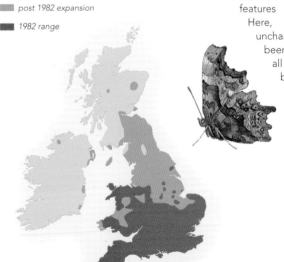

THE LIFE-CYCLE AND STRUCTURE OF A BUTTERFLY

Every butterfly goes through four very different stages during its life. It starts as an *egg* which hatches to produce a minute *caterpillar*. This feeds and grows enormously before changing into a *chrysalis*, from which the final stage, the adult *butterfly*, later emerges. Before dying, female adults lay many eggs to begin a new generation of butterflies. Some species take a whole year to complete this cycle, others fit in two, three, or even four generations between spring and autumn, but as winter approaches, all butterflies must hibernate or die. Hibernation can occur in any stage of the life-cycle but, with the exception of the Speckled Wood, the stage used is always constant for a particular species.

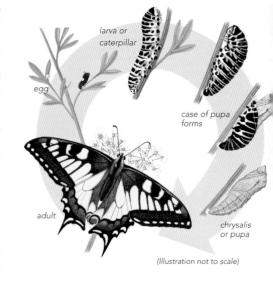

larva or caterpillar

egg

case of pupa forms

adult

chrysalis or pupa

(Illustration not to scale)

▲ *The life-cycle of the Swallowtail is typical of most butterflies. The female adult lays her eggs singly on the leaves of one plant, in this case milk parsley. The eggs hatch into the larva or caterpillar, which moults several times before it is fully grown. After the final moult, a soft-bodied pupa or chrysalis is revealed whose skin hardens to form a rigid case. Within the case the tissues of the old caterpillar reorganize before the adult butterfly emerges.*

The adult

The adult's body is divided into three distinct sections: head, thorax and abdomen. The head has two eyes, two antennae used for smelling and balance, and an extendible proboscis which it uses for drinking nectar and other liquids.

The thorax is the power box that operates three pairs of legs (although the front pair is stunted in some species) and two pairs of wings. Each wing is a double layer of thin transparent membrane, stretched between rigid veins through which blood flows. Microscopic scales cover the wings, arranged rather like tiles on a roof. Many are pigmented and others reflect or refract the light, producing iridescent colours.

The wings have many uses in addition to flight. The pattern of the underwing may camouflage the adult, whilst false eyespots and tails trick enemies into believing that the vulnerable head is elsewhere. The bright colours often attract the opposite sex, and males have special scent scales on the upper forewings that produce aphrodisiacs. In addition, dark scales along the veins of many species absorb the sun's warmth and heat the blood, whereas the underwings are often shiny, allowing overheated adults to cool down by reflecting the sun.

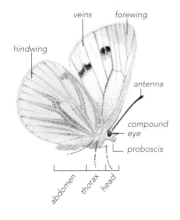

veins | forewing | hindwing | antenna | compound eye | proboscis | abdomen | thorax | head

The abdomen contains the adult's reproductive organs. After an often elaborate courtship, butterflies mate back to back (page 94) and the female later lays eggs through the tip of her abdomen (page 64).

The main activities of an adult's life are to mate and, in the case of a female, to lay as many eggs as possible in the most suitable places for their survival. Adults that hibernate also need to build up large reserves of food by drinking nectar, and before they can do anything, all adults must warm their bodies to a remarkably high temperature – around 32°C to 35°C. This they do by altering the area of wing surface exposed to the sun.

The egg, caterpillar and chrysalis

Butterfly eggs are of various shapes and sizes, as can be seen in the accounts of individual species. In detail, each consists of a hard outer shell which is particularly robust in those species that hibernate in this stage. At the top of the egg is a small depression, the micropyle, where the shell is thin, allowing oxygen to enter. Young eggs contain a mass of nutritious fluid and a microscopic embryo, which soon absorbs the fluid and grows into a little caterpillar. This nibbles its way out, often eating the whole eggshell.

The caterpillar is the main feeding stage in the life-cycle and the only one that grows. It possesses a pair of powerful jaws that are well able to chew plant leaves or flowers, in contrast to the adult which can feed only on liquids. There is a long body, bearing six true legs behind the head, four pairs of suckers (prolegs) further back, and another (the clasper) at the end. A caterpillar's skin is thin and flexible, but as the body grows, it can eventually stretch no further and is shed. By then, a new larger skin has already developed beneath the old one, often rather different in shape and colour. The number of moults in a caterpillar's life varies from three to six, depending on the species. When full grown, the skin is shed for the last time, to reveal a chrysalis underneath.

The chrysalis is the transitional stage when the caterpillar's body tissues are converted into an adult butterfly. While the hard outer case appears immobile, almost all the contents inside are being reassembled from a sort of living soup. When fully formed, the adult breaks open the chrysalis case and emerges. At first the wings are small soft pads. They are blown up by pumping blood into the veins, and will set hard after an hour or two.

▼ This Silver-studded Blue's egg is around the size of a pin-head.

▼ The Purple Emperor caterpillar is camouflaged to look like a sallow leaf.

7

COLONIES AND NUMBERS

Most British butterflies live in discrete colonies that breed in the same small areas, or close by, year after year. A typical colony fluctuates considerably in size, ranging from under 50 adults in a poor season to a few hundred in a good one. Some sites contain much larger populations of tens or even hundreds of thousands, but these are extremely unusual.

In the colony, there are generally equal numbers of males and females, although it often looks as if males predominate because the females tend to be inconspicuous. Every female present has the potential to lay several hundred eggs. In practice, 50 eggs per female is a good average, for many die before laying their full capacity. This nevertheless gives the colony an enormous potential to increase if conditions are favourable, for only two offspring need survive – to produce one male and one female – if the colony is to remain stable.

From the moment the eggs are laid it is a race against death. Unless they hibernate, typical eggs hatch after seven to ten days, by which time perhaps one in 20 will have been killed by disease, predators, or parasitic wasp larvae that are so tiny that up to 20 can develop inside a single pinhead-sized egg. Caterpillars are much more vulnerable, being killed mainly by other insects and spiders when small and by birds, shrews and mice as they grow larger. Many caterpillars are beautifully camouflaged to escape these predators; others are poisonous or have sharp spines,

Adult movements and migrations

About three-quarters of the British species live in close-knit colonies, breeding in small discrete areas from which the adults rarely stray. The other quarter are much more mobile and fly freely through the countryside, laying eggs wherever suitable conditions are encountered. These species include several of our most familiar butterflies, for example the Small Tortoiseshell and Brimstone. Some species also mix with continental populations, for example Large and Small Whites often cross the Channel, in both directions.

There are a few butterflies that regularly migrate to Britain. The Red Admiral, Painted Lady and Clouded Yellow cannot survive a British winter, except in insignificant numbers, but permanent populations breed round the Mediterranean or in North Africa. All produce vast swarms that fly north each spring to breed throughout Europe during the summer months. Some always reach southern England, and the Red Admiral is generally common. The Clouded Yellow is more sporadic, but in freak 'Clouded Yellow Years' large numbers arrive and are a common sight throughout the British Isles. There is now good evidence that migratory butterflies return south in autumn, flying at high altitudes and in larger numbers than those that arrived the previous spring. In addition to the regular migrants, there are several other species that reach Britain very rarely (page 167).

▲ *A Common Blue caterpillar eating leaves of bird's-foot trefoil while red ants milk its glands for nutritious secretions.*

and generally live in large groups which enhances this deterrent and, incidentally, makes them very easy for the naturalist to find. Unfortunately, they are equally conspicuous to parasitic wasps and flies that are not deterred by these defences and which kill vast numbers of gregarious caterpillars. Blues have a more subtle form of protection that is highly effective against predators. Nutritious liquids, from a gland and pores, ooze over their bodies and attract ants which attend them day and night, and fiercely repel any enemies.

Up to two-thirds of the caterpillars in a typical colony are killed, but this still leaves an average of about 15 from each mother that laid the original eggs to form chrysalises. Unfortunately, the chrysalis is even more prone to attack; indeed four-fifths or more of the population may be killed during this period. Birds and small mammals are again the chief culprits, and again many extraordinary forms of camouflage have evolved to combat them. Some chrysalises even live inside ant nests.

In addition to avoiding their enemies, caterpillars have to feed. Most species eat only one or a few closely related types of wild plant, and often only a certain part of the plant, for example the flowers or young leaf-tips, is palatable. Yet another requirement of some species is that they need to live in unusually warm places if they are to survive for, being cold-blooded, they take longer to develop in cool spots and this gives their enemies more time to find them. The twin needs of survival and special foodplants restrict the caterpillars of each species to living in a small and specialized part of its environment, be it in a wood, grassland or heathland.

Adult female butterflies take great care to lay eggs in the precise places where they are most likely to survive. Experienced naturalists learn exactly where to look for different species, and can often find the young stages with remarkable ease.

DISTRIBUTION AND HABITATS

Most mobile species of butterfly may be encountered almost anywhere within the British Isles, but many sedentary species have limited ranges and very patchy distributions within their ranges. This is due to the reluctance of the adults to leave their breeding grounds. Suitable sites, and hence colonies, may be few and far between, perhaps because the caterpillar's foodplant grows only on particular soils, or because it can survive only in hot places in the south. There is a noticeable fall in the number of species as one travels north, and islands also tend to have fewer butterflies.

WOODLAND

Woods differ enormously in the number of butterflies they contain. The richest examples have 35–40 different species, yet many are depressing places with no more than a few of the commonest butterflies. Some of these differences reflect geology and geography. Regional differences are small, however, when compared with the high degree of local variation that often occurs between woods in the same neighbourhood. The extent to which a wood fulfils the potential for its region depends, very largely, on its internal structure and on how it has been managed.

All woods, even the shadiest, attract up to 12 mobile species which arrive periodically to feed on flowers. Three – the Clouded Yellow, Large and Small Whites – never breed there, but the rest lay eggs if their foodplants are encountered, before moving on. These latter butterflies include the Brimstone, Comma, Peacock and Holly Blue.

The other 30 species that can be found in woods are more sedentary and will be present only if the site contains enough of the caterpillar's foodplant, growing under the right conditions, to support a whole colony year after year.

The precise places used for breeding are described under the accounts of individual species, and are summarized in the illustration opposite. Rather surprisingly, the caterpillars of only four butterflies feed on trees, while another six species eat different kinds of shrubs and climbers. In contrast, no fewer than 33 butterflies breed on various low-growing plants on the forest floor. These ground-living butterflies can roughly be divided into two groups: those that need fresh clearings where their food-plants briefly flourish before being shaded out again, and those that breed in rides, glades and wood edges. The first group includes several characteristic woodland butterflies, notably those Fritillaries that depend on a flush of violets for breeding. Look for the Pearl-bordered Fritillary in the most recent and sunniest openings in May; for the rather similar Small Pearl-bordered Fritillary two weeks later in damper spots and in slightly older clearings; and for the magnificent Silver-washed Fritillary in July in half-shaded compartments where a few taller trees remain after thinning.

In contrast, woodland rides, glades and edges are no more than sheltered strips of permanent grassland, and they support some typically grassland butterflies, for example the Browns and golden Skippers. The Speckled Wood and Ringlet are especially characteristic of woods: the former breeds along the semi-shaded edges whilst the Ringlet needs sunnier spaces that are damp and overgrown with tall grass. For a few butterflies the distinction between woodland clearings and grassland is less clear-cut: Common Blue, Wood White, Small Copper, Grizzled and Dingy Skipper can live in rides, but all do better in regenerating clearings.

In recent years, modern methods of forestry have transformed the structure of many woods and this, in turn, has caused dramatic changes in the status of several woodland butterflies. Clearings, nowadays, tend to be few and far between, and the floors of most woods are very much shadier than in the past, when practices such as coppicing

Breeding Sites in Woodlands

Fresh clearings
Dingy Skipper
Grizzled Skipper
Wood White
Small Copper
Common Blue
Duke of Burgundy

Fritillaries
Pearl-bordered
Small Pearl-bordered
High Brown
Heath
Silver-washed

Rides and glades
Chequered Skipper
Small Skipper
Essex Skipper
Large Skipper
Green-veined White
Orange Tip
Painted Lady
Red Admiral
Small Tortoiseshell
Peacock
Comma
Speckled Wood
Wall Brown
Scotch Argus
Marbled White
Gatekeeper
Ringlet
Meadow Brown
Small Heath
Marsh Fritillary
Dark Green Fritillary

Shrubs
White Admiral
Brimstone
Holly Blue
Green Hairstreak
Brown Hairstreak
Black Hairstreak

Trees
Purple Emperor
Purple Hairstreak
White-letter Hairstreak
Large Tortoiseshell

created a constant supply of fresh openings. This has had a catastrophic effect on Fritillaries and other sun-loving butterflies that need fresh ground. On the other hand, modern rides are often kept wide for large vehicles, and many so-called 'grassland' butterflies still flourish in woods that have lost their 'woodland' species. Indeed, in many flat landscapes where farming is intensive – most notably in East Anglia and the Midlands – woodland rides are now the main places to see 'grassland' butterflies. Most of the butterflies that breed on shrubs are holding their own in modern woods, but those that need deciduous trees have been greatly harmed by the switch to conifers, while Dutch elm disease has caused declines in the White-letter Hairstreak. On the credit side, the Speckled Wood and White Admiral prefer slightly shaded conditions, and these beautiful butterflies have been spreading in British woods.

▲ Coppiced woodland, where small areas of shrubs are cut back every year, provides ideal breeding sites for several scarce woodland butterflies. The blue patches of violets and bluebell were cut two years earlier and are perfect for Duke of Burgundy, Pearl-bordered and Small Pearl-bordered Fritillaries.

Butterfly watching in woods
It follows from the above that the finest woods for butterflies are large forest complexes that have a history of recent clearings, a considerable diversity of structure, and many sunny areas. On the whole, deciduous woods are much better than conifers, although young plantations on ancient sites may briefly support an abundance of rare species.

Egg-laying females tend to be inconspicuous, and the best places to watch butterflies are not necessarily where breeding occurs. Most species congregate in sunny rides and glades where, in season, scores of Browns, Skippers, Nymphalids and perhaps Fritillaries jostle for nectar. Some have favourite flowers: the short-tongued Gatekeeper prefers ragwort or fleabane whereas Brimstone and Peacock can reach down the long tubes of teasels. Everything likes Bramble, and it is much easier to wait by a sunny patch and let the butterflies come to you. At other times of the day or year, the same species that are seen on flowers will be more interested in finding mates, and this takes them into different parts of the wood. The males of most species either patrol the rides or perch in wait for females, and you will soon discover the characteristic places used by each. In slightly shaded areas, look for the male Speckled Wood as he perches in a sunbeam or indulges in a dancing flight there.

Much will be missed if butterfly watching is confined to eye level. Several species live mainly on the canopy, and binoculars are essential to see these properly. Stand in a glade where the bushy treetops are visible, and perhaps you will see a Hairstreak looping briefly above the canopy in a rapid tumbling flight. Sometimes, they can be dislodged by tapping the lowest boughs, but many more are seen if you climb a tall tree and gaze down over the treetops. There, in the richest woods, Meadow Browns, Gatekeepers, Speckled Woods, Hairstreaks, White Admirals and Large Fritillaries will also be seen crawling over the uppermost leaves, drinking the sweet honeydew secreted by aphids. Most spectacular of all, although very scarce, is the master tree of a Purple Emperor colony. The males congregate from wide areas on to a prominent tree, often an oak, and perch on particular twigs, frequently ascending to battle in violent clashing flights.

The eggs and caterpillars of several woodland butterflies are easier to find than the adult. They are up to 50 times more numerous than the adult stage, and have the benefit of being visible in the evening, in dull as well as in fine weather, and extend the field season round the whole year. Brown and Purple Hairstreaks are especially simple to find as eggs during winter by searching, respectively, the dark bare twigs of low-growing blackthorns along sheltered edges or the plump flowering-buds of oaks on the sunny side of a woodland tree. Details and practical hints on how to find all species are given in the individual accounts.

▼ The grey egg of the Purple Hairstreak is easy to find during winter by examining plump oak buds on the sunny side of a wood.

GRASSLAND

Grasslands of one type or another cover most of the British Isles and are the main breeding grounds for the majority of our species. Unfortunately, a high proportion of fields in the lowlands has been ruined for butterflies by agricultural improvement. This eliminates all the native plants on which caterpillars depend. At best, only Clouded Yellows can breed there, using sown Clovers.

Entomologists soon learn to concentrate on 'natural' grassland that has never been sprayed or reseeded. Vast acreages still survive in northern uplands and moors (pages 18–19); but in the south, breeding sites have largely been reduced to verges, woodland rides, the coastline, Army Ranges, and steep hillsides. The variety of butterflies to be found there varies with the geology, local climate, topography and soil. Richest of all grasslands are the south-facing slopes of chalk and limestone hills. This is due partly to their calcareous soils, which support a range of caterpillar foodplants that are rare or absent elsewhere, and partly to their warm aspects, which provide rare breeding sites for species like the Adonis Blue, which are better adapted to the hot climate of central Europe.

Management also has a crucial influence on the range of butterflies that is present. Fields soon revert to coarse grass and scrub if not periodically mown or grazed. There is a succession of species that flourish in swards of different heights and densities.

Very few butterflies breed in arid sun-baked turf that is really short or sparse, but for the Large Blue, Adonis Blue, Silver-spotted Skipper and Grayling this is essential. A wide range of Blues and other typical downland species inhabit grassland that is only slightly taller. All are gradually shaded out, together with their foodplants, once the turf exceeds 8 cm or so in height. Then other species proliferate: most Browns flourish in medium to tall grassland, and they in turn are replaced by several Skippers in very overgrown swards that are dominated by tussocks of coarse grasses.

The richest grasslands are those that have a varied topography, including shelter, and a patchwork of grass heights, with short thin-soiled slopes interspersed between medium and tall areas. This occurs naturally on eroding undercliffs, and often in abandoned quarries and pits. It has also been created, with breathtaking success, by selective grazing on some nature reserves. Such diversity is unusual, however, in most unimproved grassland, which is either farmed or abandoned. In the past, short open swards predominated due to intensive rabbit grazing. After myxomatosis in the 1950s, the swards grew to the opposite extreme. Countless colonies of Blues and other 'short grass' species disappeared, but Browns and some Skippers

▲ *Ant hills and an abundance of wild flowers are sure signs that this unimproved grassland is a rich breeding place for butterflies.*

became abundant. Since the 1980s, there has been a gradual return of rabbits, and today a rich mixture of short and taller turf has been recreated on many unfertilized downs. Rabbit grazing, warmer spring temperatures, agri-environment schemes, and targeted conservation grazing using domestic livestock are together responsible for the welcome recovery of the Adonis Blue and Silver-spotted Skipper – butterflies that were declining rapidly towards extinction in Britain by the late 1970s.

Blue butterflies and ants

A remarkable trait in our nine species of Blue – and in their relatives the Green, Brown and Purple Hairstreaks – is the often intricate relationship their caterpillars and chrysalids have with ants. This is so characteristic in Adonis, Chalkhill and Silver-studded Blues, and in both Brown Arguses, that the easiest way to find a caterpillar is to scan suitable growth forms of the foodplant until you spot a frenzied group of ants, then look for a beautifully camouflaged caterpillar beneath them. Similarly, the elusive chrysalids of most Blues and these Hairstreaks are best found by gently excavating the surface cells of red, black or yellow meadow ant nests.

Caterpillars and chrysalids of Lycaenid butterflies attract ants because they secrete sugars and amino acids in such large quantities that, in strong populations, they provide a major source of food for the ant colony. In return, ants tend and protect young butterflies constantly, especially during the vulnerable periods of moulting. Furthermore, the caterpillars and chrysalids produce eerie clicking sounds – easily audible to the human ear in the case of a Green Hairstreak chrysalis – that mimic the calls of adult ants. Famous among these relationships is the bizarre Large Blue (page 108) whose caterpillar feeds on ant grubs. Less well known is the Silver-studded Blue, found more often on southern heathlands than in grassland. Here, the female Blue lays her eggs around the edges of black ant (*Lasius niger*) nests. The tiny caterpillars are carried into the nests, and although they emerge at dusk to feed on various plants, they never escape their ant keepers. Equally remarkable, the adult butterfly, after emerging from its chrysalis inside a black ant nest, is smothered by ants for an hour or two while it inflates and hardens its wings. This event is best experienced by searching for agitated ants between 8.00 am and 10.00 am on strong Silver-studded Blue colonies.

▼ *Black ants tend the Silver-studded Blue while it hardens its wings after emerging from a chrysalis that was formed in the upper chambers of their ant nest.*

BUTTERFLY WATCHING IN GRASSLAND

Grassland is best explored in warm still weather, for most butterflies are grounded on windy days. The males of several species gather towards the bases of hills and in sheltered hollows, where they await females. All behave rather differently there: certain Blues and Browns will be found settled on the ground, others patrol backwards and forwards. The Green Hairstreak, Duke of Burgundy and Large Skipper establish individual perching posts on prominent branches of shrubs, or tall tussocks. Any male is easy to approach and photograph on his perching post. He remains in position for hours, invariably returning to the same twig or leaf when disturbed.

Blue butterflies are among the chief delights of southern chalk and limestone hills. Five grassland species may be present on the best sites, as well as the Holly Blue if shrubs or trees are present. The Brown Argus is the first to emerge, and by late May Common, Adonis and Small Blues are also well out, together with their close relatives, the Small Copper and Green Hairstreak. These six Lycaenids last well into June. There is then a lull before the first Chalkhill Blues emerge. August provides another magnificent display with the Chalkhills, then at their peak, joined by second broods of Brown Argus, and Common and Adonis Blues. There may be tens of thousands of Blues flying together on exceptional

▼ *The Marbled White is often abundant in late June and July on high-quality downs in southern England.*

▲ *A group of Chalkhill Blues bask in the evening sunlight before roosting overnight on grass stems and kidney vetch seedheads.*

sites. Dingy Skipper, Small Heath and Wall also emerge in May followed by further broods of the last two species in August and September. In contrast, the majority of Browns and Skippers fly in July and August, amply compensating for the temporary lack of Blues.

In season, male and female Blues can be found in the early evening, roosting in groups on tall grass clumps, again usually in sheltered hollows or along the bases of hills. There may be large numbers on each clump, sometimes consisting of several species, more often each in its own group. Roosts are easy to find by crouching and scanning the grassheads at eye level. It is well worth watching one in the morning when it is first exposed to full sunshine. For a few minutes, every adult basks with its wings wide open before dispersing. Early morning and late afternoon are the best times to photograph both Blues and Browns; during the heat of the day, most sit with their wings half or completely closed, and Browns, in particular, are hard to approach.

The young stages can also be found once one has learned the plants and situations chosen for egg-laying. Start with easy species such as the eggs of Duke of Burgundy, Small Copper and most Blues. Blue caterpillars are best discovered by scanning the foodplant for ants (see page 15). Brown caterpillars hide deep in grass clumps by day, but ascend to eat the tender leaf tips after dark. They can easily be spotted by torchlight. Different grasses, growing in particular places, will yield different species; all are easy to rear, as are Blue caterpillars with or without ants.

HEATHS, MOORS, BOGS AND MOUNTAINS

These wild treeless habitats support a small but distinctive range of butterflies, including several species that are rare or absent elsewhere.

Heaths are open areas in lowland Britain, where ancient forest clearances have left sandy exposures too poor to develop into true grassland. Most heaths are dominated by heathers, and support a limited number of low-growing plants, with few grasses except in the wetter areas. In late summer Small Tortoiseshell, Painted Lady, and other Vanessids are attracted to the flowering heather, but seldom breed there. Characteristic breeding species include Small Heath, Gatekeeper, Common Blue, Small Copper and Green Hairstreak, but all are commonest where the land has been disturbed and, to some extent, enriched. There are, however, two butterflies that are especially characteristic of pure heathland: Grayling and Silver-studded Blue. Graylings live in the driest spots where there are patches of exposed sand and sparse tufts of fine grasses on which the caterpillars feed. Although now very rare elsewhere (except on coastal dunes that resemble heaths), this large grey butterfly remains the characteristic Brown of lowland heathland. Much more localized, and almost confined to southern heaths, is the Silver-studded Blue. This beautiful Blue can occur in vast numbers after a fire or clearing, for the caterpillars feed on the tender growths of regenerating plants in spots where black ant nests are abundant (page 15). Search also in moister areas where the heather has grown leggy.

Moors are similar to heaths, but occur at higher altitudes and mainly in the north, where the climate is colder and wetter. Bogs develop among poorly drained moorland, and can occur in small pockets on lowland heaths. These are waterlogged areas that are grassy round the edges, merging into wetter regions of pure moss that often surround open water. Moors and bogs dominate the sides of many mountains, but there

▼ *The Grayling is the characteristic Brown of dry southern heaths, where fine grasses and bell heather abound.*

▲ *The beautiful* davus *race of the Large Heath, seen here on cross-leaved heath, is a local inhabitant of northern bogs.*

may also be lush grassy meadows degenerating at high altitudes into a barren landscape of broken rocks.

The few butterflies that live in these upland habitats are adapted to withstand intense cold during winter and, in some cases, the prolonged submergence of their caterpillars. Some, like the Chequered Skipper, Marsh and Dark Green Fritillary have evolved beautiful races with large dusky wings that are better able to absorb the sun's rays.

The Large Heath is an attractive butterfly that lives only in the wettest acid bogs; search where cotton grass is abundant at all altitudes up to 800 m (2,600 ft). Less waterlogged areas, where purple moor grass is dominant, are the habitat of the Marsh Fritillary, Chequered Skipper and Scotch Argus. These two latter butterflies are virtually confined, nowadays, to Scotland, and are found especially near plantations or among scrub, at altitudes of up to about 500 m (1,650 ft). Our most truly mountain species is the Mountain Ringlet which breeds only in lush meadows from 350–1,000 m (1,150–3,300 ft) high in the English Lake District and Scottish Highlands. Its very dark wings are particularly adept at absorbing the sun's warmth, as are those of another relic from the Ice Age, the Northern Brown Argus. This lives at lower altitudes, up to 350 m (1,150 ft), and is confined to well-drained base-rich northern hillsides, where rockroses or geraniums are common.

GARDENS AND HEDGEROWS

Large numbers of adult butterflies are attracted to gardens, but the range of species is small because few are able to breed there. Since Fritillaries, Hairstreaks and most Blues, Browns and Skippers seldom leave their breeding sites, it is unusual to see any in towns or suburbs. Favoured country gardens will support low densities of Speckled Wood, Meadow Brown and Large Skipper, but they usually attract only odd individuals of the other sedentary butterflies from colonies that happen to occur nearby. However, all the more mobile species are attracted to garden flowers, notably the five common Vanessids: the Small Tortoiseshell, Peacock, Red Admiral, Comma and Painted Lady (pages 36–38). All have increased in abundance in recent years due to warmer weather and an increase in nettles, and the Comma, in particular, has spread north. Consequently, all five species are attracted to gardens over a far wider range of the British Isles than was the case three decades ago. The Small Tortoiseshell also often hibernates in cool lofts, garages or outhouses.

The second commonest group of garden butterflies are the Whites. Only the Large and Small White, together known as Cabbage Whites, regularly breed there, but for them the vegetable patch is a major breeding ground. Both are seen from spring until late autumn, reaching a peak in August when they have a penchant for lavender flowers. Orange Tips and Green-veined Whites are also frequent visitors, but although the male Orange Tip is unmistakable, females and Green-veined Whites are often overlooked as Small Whites; at rest, the green mottling and lines on their respective underwings make both easy to identify. Planting lady's smock, or the less attractive garlic mustard, are sure ways of attracting these lovely Whites to breed in your garden: the orange eggs and blue-green caterpillars of the Orange Tip are especially beautiful and easily found on the flowerbuds and seed pods of both plants.

The Holly Blue is the only other species to breed significantly in gardens. Uniquely among British Blues, it is common in many suburbs, supported wholly by garden shrubs.

Hedgerows are much more important habitats. There is seldom an abundance of adults present, but the range of species can be considerable. Indeed, in intensively farmed flat landscapes, hedges and occasional woods are the main places left for breeding butterflies, whilst in Britain as a whole, the majority of Brown Hairstreak, Gatekeeper, Peacock, Comma, Holly Blue, Green-veined White, Orange Tip and Brimstone caterpillars feed either on hedgerow shrubs or on the ground plants beneath hedges. In winter, search

▶ *The Brown Hairstreak is one of the few butterflies that breeds largely on hedgerows in Britain. The adult is secretive, but its white eggs are easily found on bare blackthorn twigs in winter.*

blackthorn twigs for the conspicuous white eggs of Brown Hairstreaks (page 82). In early spring, adult Peacock, Small Tortoiseshell, Comma and Brimstone provide the main show, feeding first on flowers after winter hibernation before their males establish territories and the females search for egg sites. Soon they are joined by Orange Tip, Green-veined White and Holly Blue, all having emerged from overwintering chrysalises. Last to appear are the butterflies that hibernated in hedge-banks as caterpillars, then eggs. These include Small Copper, Common Blue, Large and Small Skippers and several Browns, which provide a growing spectacle that climaxes with the flowering of brambles and (in the south) the emergence of the Gatekeeper. The finale to the season is the return of Vanessids and Brimstones to feed on late flowers and weeping blackberries, whilst any ditch containing fleabane is sure to attract late-flying Browns and the last generations of Common Blue and Small Copper.

The best hedges to search for butterflies are ancient boundaries that contain a variety of shrubs growing above a sheltered bank or broad verge containing a rich ground flora. Spraying, ploughing, or burning the verge up to the edge greatly reduces the number of butterflies, as does frequent and severe trimming of the shrubs; tall unkempt hedges that are left two to four years between cuttings are ideal.

GARDEN PLANTS FOR BUTTERFLIES

It is simple to attract all the species of mobile butterfly in the neighbourhood merely by growing their favourite nectar sources. It is much harder to create suitable conditions for breeding (except for Holly Blue, Large and Small Whites), but well worth trying; even if you fail, Whites, Yellows and others will remain longer in the garden if their caterpillars' foodplants are present.

There are a few simple rules: try to create a suntrap where banks of flowers grow in full sunshine and yet have maximum shelter from the wind; only a limited range of garden flowers is really attractive to butterflies – aim for a succession of these from early spring until late autumn, and ensure that

there is a profusion from mid-summer onwards when the Vanessids and Brimstones arrive to feed before hibernating; old-fashioned varieties and species of plants are infinitely superior to most modern varieties. This is particularly true of the best of all butterfly plants, *Buddleia davidii*: the wild unkempt shrub with pale mauve flowers will fill any garden with the scent of honey and often be smothered with butterflies, as will the later-flowering dwarf Beijing buddleia, but many modern dark red and purple varieties, although neater, are virtually scentless and seldom attract anything.

▼ *From mid-summer onwards buddleia attracts large numbers of Vanessids, such as the Small Tortoiseshell and Peacock, which feed on its rich nectar before hibernating over winter.*

Definitive lists of attractive plants are given in two delightful books, Chris Baines' *How to Make a Wildlife Garden* and Margaret Vickery's *Gardening for Butterflies*. I recommend flowering sallow (pussy willow) and crocus for early spring, followed by wallflower, and wild species of primrose, bugle and forget-me-not. Sweet rocket and lady's smock are excellent flowers for all Whites, especially Green-veined and Orange Tip, which may also be attracted, in diminishing order, by horse radish, honesty, *Arabis* and aubretia. They will sometimes lay eggs, Green-veined on young leaves and Orange Tip on the flowers, of all these crucifers.

By June and July, a good garden for butterflies should have sweet william, thyme and candytuft in flower, followed by applemint, marjoram, wild hemp agrimony (*Eupatorium cannabium*), red valerian, lavender, verbena, and above all the two great shrubs: buddleia and hebe. The former will flower from mid-July until late September if some branches are pruned hard in spring. Two essential plants for autumn are ice plant (ensure that it is *Sedum spectabile*) and Michaelmas daisy, whilst rotten fruit left lying on the ground is irresistible to Red Admirals.

Like it or not, any vegetable patch containing brassicas will attract Small and Large Whites; cabbages, Brussels sprouts and also garden nasturtiums are especially favoured for breeding. Brimstones have an extraordinary ability to find purging and alder buckthorns; one bush in a hedge is ample and will attract many more adults in spring than garden flowers. Holly Blues seldom feed on flowers, but can be attracted to breed in any garden that has flowering (female) holly in spring or ivy in summer. Variegated varieties of both are suitable, provided they flower and fruit in sunny sheltered spots. Finally, stinging nettle is invaluable as the foodplant of four Vanessids, but note that it is unlikely to be used unless growing on the sheltered, sunny side of a hedge or wall, and unless young growth is available; it is possible to create a succession of fresh leaves by occasional cuttings in spring and early summer.

BUTTERFLY OR MOTH?

Butterflies and moths form a large group of related insects, the *Lepidoptera*, which differ from all other insects in having wings that are covered with minute, overlapping scales. Another unique feature is the adult's proboscis: a long tube for a mouth, which is normally kept coiled beneath the head but can be extended like a straw to drink liquids. About 2,400 species of *Lepidoptera* are regularly found in Britain, but only 60 of these are butterflies; the rest are moths. With practice, it is easy to distinguish between the two groups, although there are few hard and fast rules.

All butterflies fly during the day and most are brightly coloured; moths tend to be nocturnal and many are rather drab. British butterflies have quite thin bodies and, with the exception of the Dingy Skipper, shut their wings together above the body when they rest. Many moths are fat and furry, and settle in various postures, often with the wings draped round the body. There are, nevertheless, several day-flying moths, some of which are highly coloured (pages 170–171). The surest way to distinguish between these and butterflies is to examine the antennae (feelers): those of butterflies are slender and always end in a swollen tip or club. Only Burnet moths (below) have anything approaching clubbed antennae; these are conspicuous, familiar insects that are as easy to identify as butterflies. The antennae of other moths come in a rich array of shapes ranging from single strands to intricate feathers.

▼ *The day-flying Six-spot Burnet resembles a butterfly, but like many moths drapes its wings around a fat furry body.*

HOW TO USE THE FIELD GUIDE

Sixty species of butterfly, from six different families, are regularly seen in Britain. On the whole, the members of each group share strong family characteristics and differ rather obviously from butterflies in different families. The main family groups are illustrated on pages 26–27. For convenience, the large Nymphalid family has been split into three, and the Duke of Burgundy has been added to the similar-looking Fritillaries, although it really belongs to a family on its own.

Having identified the family group from the illustrations on these pages, turn to the appropriate identification notes and illustrations on the family group pages. Here all the members of each group are illustrated life-size, with notes pointing out features that help to distinguish between them.

Also included for each group is a chart of adult flight periods. The thickness of the red line represents the relative numbers of each species likely to be out through the summer months. Opposite this is a summary of each butterfly's status in the four countries. The symbols mean:

Common and widespread
Local
Scarce
Rare

♂ Male
♀ Female

When you have decided what you think the butterfly is, follow the reference to the double-page spread for that species, where a more detailed description of the distinctive features of both sexes will confirm your identification or point you in another direction.

GUIDE TO THE MAIN FAMILY GROUPS

Skippers (Hesperiidae)

Pages 28–29

Small and moth-like, Skippers live in discrete colonies in rough unfertilized grassland. Adults rarely stray and are often hidden among vegetation. Flight, when it occurs, is rapid and whirring, 'skipping' just above the grassheads. Most species have golden wings, but three are grey or chequered in black, white or yellow.

antennae held wide apart, usually hooked at tips

head as wide as body

large broad body

large black eyes

short stumpy wings, often held apart in golden Skippers

Swallowtail (Papilionidae)

Page 39

Large black and yellow with tails. Unmistakable.

Yellows and Whites (Pieridae)

Pages 30–32

Medium-sized to fairly large, with white or yellow wings, a few black marks, and a little green or orange in one or two species. The Marbled White (a 'Brown') and Swallowtail also fit this description, but both are highly distinctive. True Whites have slow fluttering flights; all but Wood Whites roam fairly freely through the countryside, occurring in ones or twos in most habitats.

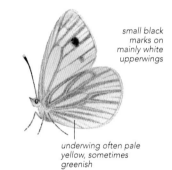

small black marks on mainly white upperwings

underwing often pale yellow, sometimes greenish

Copper, Hairstreaks and Blues (Lycaenidae)

Pages 33–35

Small butterflies, most with bright metallic colours. The Small Copper is unmistakable; 'Blues' include all butterflies with blue upperwings, though some females and a few males are brown. Coppers and Blues have numerous small spots on the underwings; all are active and conspicuous, and all except the Holly Blue live in discrete colonies in open, usually short, unfertilized grass or heathland. The Holly Blue wanders and prefers shrubs.

Hairstreaks are elusive, living in small compact colonies, mostly on treetops. All except the Green Hairstreak have tails.

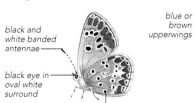

black and white banded antennae

black eye in oval white surround

blue or brown upperwings

spots on underwings

The aristocrats: Vanessids, Emperor and Admirals (Nymphalinae, Apaturinae and Limenitinae)

Pages 36–38

Medium-sized to large, with powerful flitting flights. Vanessids have indented wing edges and bright and gaudy upperwings, mainly coloured orange, black or red. Some also have small blue or white marks. The underwings are sombre, camouflaged to resemble bark or dead leaves. All are seen in small numbers in most habitats, including gardens. The Purple Emperor and White Admiral have large dark upperwings banded in white. They live in discrete colonies in large woods.

jagged edges to wings

black marks contrast bright orange or reddish upperwings

only two pairs of walking legs

dull underwings like bark or a dead leaf

Fritillaries (Argynninae)

Pages 40–42

True Fritillaries are medium-sized to large butterflies with bright orange or golden upperwings criss-crossed by a network of black veins, crossbars, and often spots. The underwings are less golden but often intricately patterned; most species have bands of silver or white cells. They have a flitting flight. The Duke of Burgundy has a similar pattern, but is small with a whirring flight. All live in discrete colonies, mainly in woods.

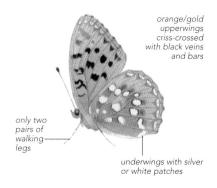

orange/gold upperwings criss-crossed with black veins and bars

only two pairs of walking legs

underwings with silver or white patches

Browns (Satyrinae)

Pages 43–45

Small to fairly large, with a conspicuous black eyespot near the tip of the forewing on both sides. This nearly always has a white centre; similar eyespots often occur elsewhere on wings. The ground colour is generally tawny, light or dark brown, except on the Marbled White (black and white) and Wall Brown (golden, like a Fritillary with eyespots). Browns live in discrete colonies, usually in tall grassland, and flap lazily just above the grasslands.

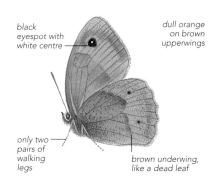

black eyespot with white centre

dull orange on brown upperwings

only two pairs of walking legs

brown underwing, like a dead leaf

SKIPPERS

There are eight species. Narrow these down to four or fewer possibilities from the date and place; then decide between Group A or Group B and see opposite. Finally, check in the fuller accounts of individual species (pages 46–61).

Mar	Apr	May	Jun	Jul	Aug	Sep	Oct/Nov		England	Wales	Scotland	Ireland
		◆			—			Grizzled	■	●		
		◆			—			Dingy	■	■	○	●
		◆						Chequered			○	
			◆					Large			○	
			◆					Small				
				◆				Essex		○		○
				◆				Lulworth	○			
					◆			Silver-spotted	○			

Group A

Bask with each fore and hindwing held together in the same plane, often flat. Predominantly dark wings with clear-cut white or yellow markings in some species. Mainly May or June. Over by mid-July.

Group B

Bask with the forewings held aloft and the hindwings more horizontal. Predominantly golden wings with rather indistinct markings in some species. Rarely seen before June.

Group A

brown wings and fringe

uniform underside

black and white pattern on wings and fringe

patterned underside

Dingy Skipper Page 58

Grizzled Skipper Page 60

yellow and black chequered pattern can be confused with the Duke of Burgundy

Central west Scotland only and the only Skipper in this region

Chequered Skipper Page 46

Group B

tip of antenna orange underneath

clear gold upper and undersides in both sexes

tip of antenna black underneath

long, thick, oblique scent mark (♂ only)

short thin scent mark parallel to veins (♂ only)

Small Skipper Page 48

Essex Skipper Page 50

dull orange to olive upperparts

circle of gold spots

only found near coast of Dorset

Lulworth Skipper Page 52

faint pattern on underside

greenish underside with silver spots

rare on chalk downs in southern England

Large Skipper Page 56

Silver-spotted Skipper Page 54

WHITE BUTTERFLIES

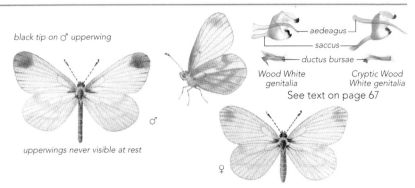

black tip on ♂ upperwing

upperwings never visible at rest

♂

aedeagus
saccus
ductus bursae

Wood White
genitalia

Cryptic Wood
White genitalia

See text on page 67

♀

Wood White and Cryptic Wood White Pages 64 and 66

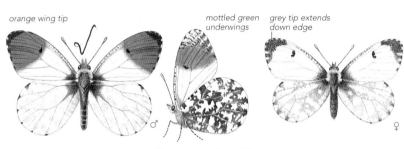

orange wing tip

mottled green underwings

grey tip extends down edge

♂

♀

Orange Tip Page 78

black down edge

spring ♂ has heavily veined underwings as in ♀

♂

heavily marked upperwing in summer

faintly veined underwing in summer

♀

Green-veined White Page 76

black tip extends down the side

spots on ♀ upperwing, none on ♂

Large White Page 72

one or no central black spot on ♂

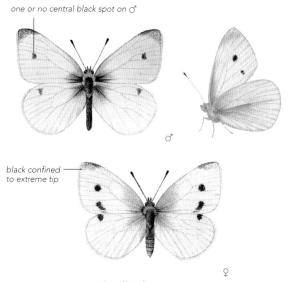

black confined to extreme tip

Small White Page 74

YELLOWS AND WHITES

	Mar	Apr	May	Jun	Jul	Aug	Sep	Oct/Nov		England	Wales	Scotland	Ireland
									Brimstone		■		●
									Clouded Yellow	■	●	○	●
									Green-veined White				
									Small White				
									Orange Tip			■	
									Large White				
									Wood White	○	○		○
									Cryptic Wood White				■

See page 43 for Marbled White.

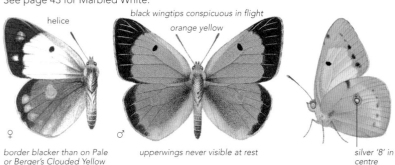

helice

black wingtips conspicuous in flight

orange yellow

♀
border blacker than on Pale or Berger's Clouded Yellow

♂
upperwings never visible at rest

silver '8' in centre

Clouded Yellow Page 68

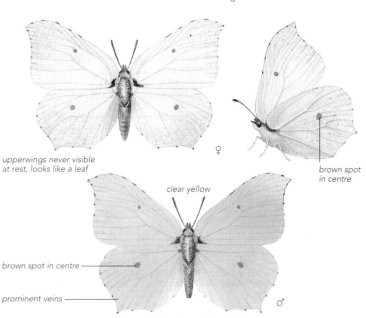

upperwings never visible at rest, looks like a leaf

♀

brown spot in centre

clear yellow

brown spot in centre

prominent veins

♂

Brimstone Page 70

Mar	Apr	May	Jun	Jul	Aug	Sep	Oct		England	Wales	Scotland	Ireland
								Small Copper	▧	▧	■	■
								Green Hairstreak	■	■	●	●
								Black Hairstreak	○			
								White-letter H'stk	●	●		
								Purple Hairstreak	■	■	●	○
								Brown Hairstreak	●	●		○

Small Copper Page 90
short tails

Green Hairstreak Page 80
tail short or absent

eye

Purple Hairstreak Page 84

Brown Hairstreak Page 82

angular wingtip

rounded wingtip

no spots

row of spots

White-letter Hairstreak Page 86

Black Hairstreak Page 88

BLUES

All species except the Holly Blue are colonial, so usually males and females will both be present, looking different in most species. Upperwing colour is a poor guide except in male Adonis and Chalkhill Blues. Check upperwings for broad/narrow black borders and spots, fringes for black veins, and underwings for absence (Group A) or presence (Group B) of orange, and the size and pattern of spots.

Mar	Apr	May	Jun	Jul	Aug	Sep	Oct			England	Wales	Scotland	Ireland
							—		Holly Blue		■	○	●
									Brown Argus	■	●		
									Common Blue				
				—					Small Blue	●	○	○	●
									Adonis Blue	●			
									Nthn. Brown Argus	○		●	
									Large Blue	○			
									Silver-studded Blue	●	○		
									Chalkhill Blue	■			

Group A No orange on underwings or upperwings.

spots

broad black margin
Large Blue Page 108

♀ has brown upperwings with no blue

silver underwings with minute black dots

Small Blue Page 92

chequered upperwing fringe
violet

silver underwings with tiny black dots

broad black margin

clear hindwing fringe

round shrubs and in gardens

Holly Blue Page 106

Group B Orange mark on underwings and some upperwings.

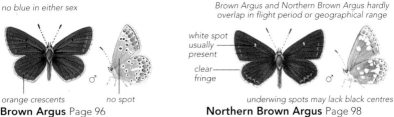

no blue in either sex

orange crescents   no spot
Brown Argus Page 96

Brown Argus and Northern Brown Argus hardly overlap in flight period or geographical range

white spot usually present

clear fringe

underwing spots may lack black centres
Northern Brown Argus Page 98

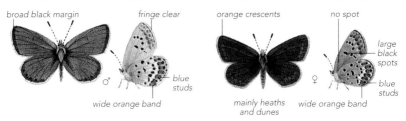

broad black margin

fringe clear

orange crescents

no spot

large black spots

blue studs

wide orange band

mainly heaths and dunes

wide orange band

blue studs

Silver-studded Blue Page 94

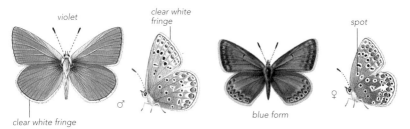

violet

clear white fringe

spot

clear white fringe

blue form

common in all habitats; all intermediates between brown and blue females exist

Common Blue Page 100

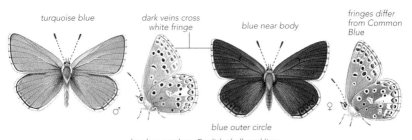

turquoise blue

dark veins cross white fringe

blue near body

fringes differ from Common Blue

blue outer circle

local on southern English chalk and lime

Adonis Blue Page 104

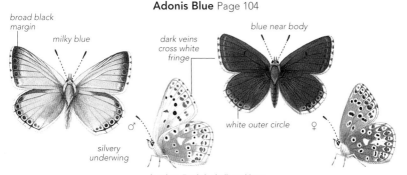

broad black margin

milky blue

dark veins cross white fringe

blue near body

silvery underwing

white outer circle

local on English chalk and lime

Chalkhill Blue Page 102

35

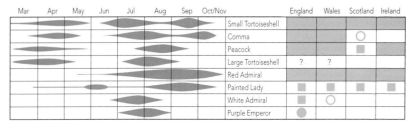

Mar	Apr	May	Jun	Jul	Aug	Sep	Oct/Nov		England	Wales	Scotland	Ireland
								Small Tortoiseshell				
								Comma			○	
								Peacock			■	
								Large Tortoiseshell	?	?		
								Red Admiral				
								Painted Lady	■	■	■	■
								White Admiral	■	○		
								Purple Emperor	●			

rounded wings

broad white band across dark upperwings

♂

bright neatly patterned underwings

White Admiral Page 112

pointed wings

eye

purple in sunshine (♂)

♂

♀ always brown

♂

♀

Purple Emperor Page 114

white spot near tip

blue marks

patterned underwings

large black area

♂

Small Tortoiseshell Page 120

no white spot

no blue on forewing

dull underwings

♂

possibly extinct

Large Tortoiseshell Page 122

no blue on forewing or hindwing

ragged wings

♂

comma mark on underwing

Comma Page 126

white patches in black tips

♂

eyespots

Painted Lady Page 118

white patches in black tip

red band

♂

Red Admiral Page 116

large eye

♂

black underwings

Peacock Page 124

Mar	Apr	May	Jun	Jul	Aug	Sep	Oct/Nov		England	Wales	Scotland	Ireland
								Swallowtail	○			

unmistakable; found in Norfolk Broads only, except for rare escapees and vagrants

Swallowtail Page 62

Mar	Apr	May	Jun	Jul	Aug	Sep	Oct		England	Wales	Scotland	Ireland
		●	●					Pearl-bordered	○	○	○	○
		●						Duke of Burgundy	○			
		●	●					Marsh	○	○	○	●
		●	●	●				Small Pearl-bordered	●	▪	▪	
		●	●					Glanville	○			
		●	●					Heath	○			
			●	●				Dark Green	●	●	●	●
			●	●				High Brown	○	○		
			●	●				Silver-washed	▪	▪		●

Medium-sized Fritillaries

spots on upper forewing

six or seven silver pearls along edge

up to six silver patches

Small Pearl-bordered Fritillary Page 128

spots on upper forewing

two silver patches

seven silver pearls

Pearl-bordered Fritillary Page 130

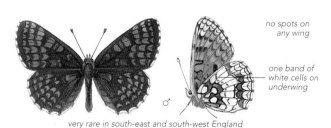

no spots on any wing

one band of white cells on underwing

very rare in south-east and south-west England

Heath Fritillary Page 142

spots on tip

bright underwings

two rows of spots

black spots in orange circles

♂

Isle of Wight only
Glanville Fritillary Page 140

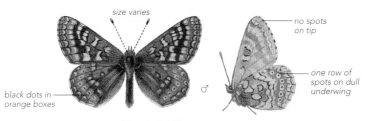

size varies

no spots on tip

one row of spots on dull underwing

black dots in orange boxes

♂

Marsh Fritillary Page 138

spots on all edges

♂

two bands of white cells on underwing

♀

Duke of Burgundy Page 110

Large Fritillaries

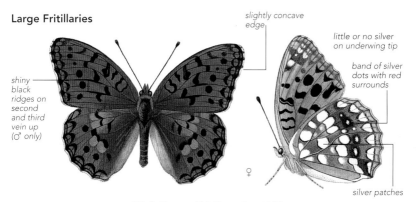

slightly concave edge

little or no silver on underwing tip

band of silver dots with red surrounds

shiny black ridges on second and third vein up (♂ only)

♀

silver patches

High Brown Fritillary Page 132

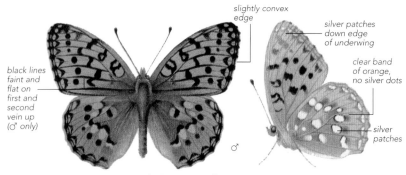

slightly convex edge

silver patches down edge of underwing

clear band of orange, no silver dots

black lines faint and flat on first and second vein up (♂ only)

silver patches

♂

Dark Green Fritillary Page 134

black streaks on upper forewing

wishy-washy silver stripes

♂

no black streaks on female's forewing

♀

valezina

♀

Silver-washed Fritillary Page 136

Mar	Apr	May	Jun	Jul	Aug	Sep	Oct		England	Wales	Scotland	Ireland
								Speckled Wood			▪	
								Wall Brown	▪	▪	○	▪
								Small Heath				▪
								Meadow Brown				
								Mountain Ringlet	○		○	
								Large Heath	○	○	▪	●
								Marbled White	▪	●		
								Ringlet			▪	
								Gatekeeper				●
								Grayling	●	●	●	●
								Scotch Argus	○		▪	

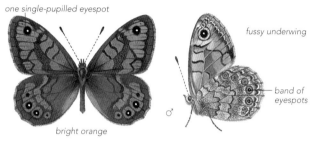

one single-pupilled eyespot

fussy underwing

band of eyespots

bright orange

Wall Brown Page 146

one single-pupilled eyespot

brown and cream

blurred underwing

Speckled Wood Page 144

unmistakable black and white chequered pattern, see Whites pages 30–31

Marbled White Page 152

never opens wings when settled

eyespots large and dark

almost no trace of eyespots

davus *form*

davus *form*

scotica *form*

Large Heath Page 162

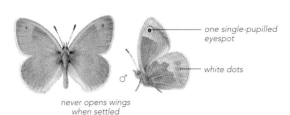

one single-pupilled eyespot

white dots

never opens wings when settled

Small Heath Page 160

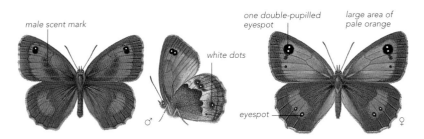

male scent mark

white dots

one double-pupilled eyespot

large area of pale orange

eyespot

♂

♀

Gatekeeper Page 156

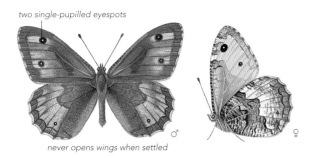

two single-pupilled eyespots

♂

♀

never opens wings when settled

Grayling Page 154

eyespot small on ♂

plain brown hindwing

one single-pupilled eyespot

less orange than Gatekeeper

black dots

♀

♂

♀

Meadow Brown Page 158

very dark

five eyespots with yellow haloes on hindwing

♂

Ringlet Page 164

faint eyespots with no white pupils

northern mountains only

♂

Mountain Ringlet Page 148

north only

two single-pupilled eyespots form '8'

♂

Scotch Argus Page 150

CHEQUERED SKIPPER *Carterocephalus palaemon*

Adult identification

Average wingspan 29 mm (♂) to 31 mm (♀)

Our only Skipper with a really distinct chequered pattern on the upperwings; note the bright orange-yellow marks among a blackish-brown background and broad veins. The female has paler marks,

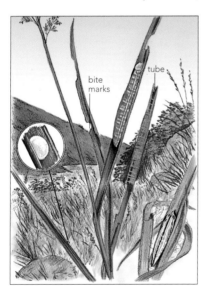

▲ *A female of the rare Chequered Skipper in a Scottish glade. It is the most distinctively marked of all the Skippers.*

but the sexes are similar: the underwings show the same clear pattern, but are duller with a greenish-grey ground colour.

In England, the Duke of Burgundy (page 110) is superficially similar in markings, size and flight, and is often mistaken for this species. At rest, the Duke of Burgundy is distinguished by a row of black spots on an orange background along all the wing edges, and its neater bands of white marks on the under hindwings. Some Carpet Moths are also similar in flight. On the continent, it may be confused with the Northern Chequered Skipper and the beautiful Large Chequered Skipper.

Young stages

The **egg** is globular and shiny white with fine reticulations. It is laid singly on a blade of purple moor grass or wood false brome and is difficult to locate.

The **caterpillar** lives in a tube formed from whichever grass the egg was laid

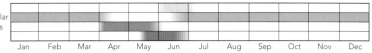

	Jan	Feb	Mar	Apr	May	Jun	Jul	Aug	Sep	Oct	Nov	Dec
egg												
caterpillar												
chrysalis												
adult												

upon, the edges being bound together by stout silk cords. The blade is eaten above and below the tube, leaving it isolated on the midrib and easy to spot from July onwards. By October, the fully fed caterpillar is green, with dark green and white lines and a pale green head. It hibernates, fully grown, in a tent of leaf blades and gradually turns straw-coloured.

The **chrysalis** is formed in spring in a new tent of dead leaf blades. It is well camouflaged, being pale buff-coloured with dark lines.

Habitat and behaviour

The adults live in small isolated colonies, and are easy to miss except in the finest weather. In England, they were once found in sunny woodland rides, clearings, and rough sheltered grassland adjoining woods, where the caterpillars fed almost wholly on wood false brome (*Brachypodium sylvaticum*). This grass is sometimes used in Scotland, but purple moor grass (*Molinea caerulea*) is the main foodplant north of the border. Search for Scottish colonies in sunny scrubby areas, often on the edges of copses or in sheltered coombs. In Scotland the eggs are laid on small clumps of grass, half-shaded by bog myrtle and other shrubs; the large exposed tussocks of purple moor grass that grow in open damp rank grassland or moorland are invariably ignored.

The adults are rather inconspicuous, but in fine weather bask with their wings wide open, and the males establish perching posts on small prominent shrubs in sunny nooks. From these they make the typical short buzzing flights of Skippers, chasing females and visiting flowers.

Distribution and status

This is a rare butterfly, now confined to a small region of west Scotland. It once occurred in several woods in north Lincolnshire and the east and southern English Midlands, but all English colonies are almost certainly now extinct, the last survivors being recorded in the mid-1970s in Rockingham Forest and other woods near Peterborough. Note that the Duke of Burgundy, with which it may be confused, occurs on some former English sites.

The Chequered Skipper was not discovered in Scotland until 1939, when a colony was found near Fort William, Inverness. Several more are now known to exist over a considerable area of Inverness and Argyll, and today one can guarantee to see it on a number of sites in this region, given suitable weather. It is not thought that the butterfly has spread or increased, merely that it had been overlooked. It is worth searching any patch of suitable habitat in this region rather than confining oneself to the well-known colonies.

confirmed range

47

SMALL SKIPPER *Thymelicus sylvestris*

Adult identification
Average wingspan 30 mm

The sexes are similar in size and appearance, apart from a black scent line across each upper forewing on the males

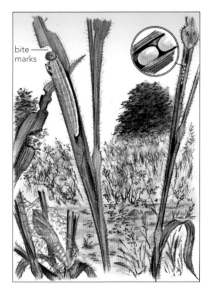

bite marks

▲ *A Small Skipper in typical basking posture. This species may be confused with the Essex Skipper, but for the reddish-orange antennae undersides.*

(page 29). The upperwings are bright orange-brown, with faint black veins and black margins. The underwings are a dull orange-brown, tinged with grey-green, and are not patterned.

The Essex Skipper often flies with this butterfly and is almost identical. It is usually necessary to net and examine the undersurfaces of the tips of the antennae: these are deep black on the Essex Skipper, as if dipped in ink, but reddish-orange on the Small Skipper (page 29). The male Small Skipper also has a longer bolder scent mark that runs obliquely, rather than parallel to the upperwing edge. See also the male Lulworth Skipper (page 29) which is smaller and less golden. No other species in Europe is similar to these three.

Young stages
Three to five smooth, pale yellow, flat-tened oval **eggs** are laid in a row inside

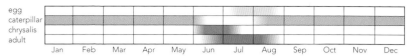

	Jan	Feb	Mar	Apr	May	Jun	Jul	Aug	Sep	Oct	Nov	Dec
egg												
caterpillar												
chrysalis												
adult												

the sheath of a tall grass stem, usually Yorkshire fog. These are quite easy to find.

The **caterpillars** hibernate together without feeding in minute silk cocoons spun in their grass sheath. In spring they disperse and live alone in rolled leaf blades fastened into a tube by silk cords. The caterpillar leaves wedge-shaped notches after feeding on other blades, which are easy to spot in May. When fully grown, it often rests exposed on leaf blades and has a green head, with a pale green body marked by darker lines on top.

The **chrysalis** is waxy green, paler on the abdomen, and has a short pink beak on the head. Look for it in a loose cocoon of coarse silk netting and grass leaves.

Habitat and behaviour

The Small Skipper forms discrete colonies from which the adults rarely stray. In the south, it occurs in most places where Yorkshire fog and wild grasses are allowed to grow tall, but it is easy to miss a small colony because the adults frequently rest among dense vegetation. Small colonies are often found along thin strips of land, such as road verges and hedge banks. Larger numbers breed along most woodland rides and edges, whilst vast populations often develop in rough abandoned or disturbed grassland.

On most sites, the main or only food of the caterpillar is Yorkshire fog (*Holcus lanatus*), although breeding sometimes occurs on timothy (*Phleum pratense*) and wood false brome (*Brachypodium sylvaticum*). The female chooses tall mature clumps around which she makes a circling buzzing flight, before crawling up and down the flowering stems, probing the loose sheaths to find one that is suitable for her eggs. Although Yorkshire fog is eliminated from intensively cultivated fields, it is common still in rough grassland, wasteland and woodland on all soils.

Distribution and status

The Small Skipper is one of the commonest and most widely distributed butterflies on all soils in England and Wales. In the past 30 years of warm weather it has spread, in a solid block, about 100 km north of its traditional boundaries, but there is still a clear-cut northern limit to its range. At present, it is absent from north-west England, Scotland and Ireland, but is expected to colonize the former two regions before 2020. In the south, numerous colonies have been eliminated through intensive farming and the removal of hedgerows, especially in flat landscapes, but it is still to be expected almost anywhere where Yorkshire fog grows in tall clumps within its range.

On the continent, it is also common and virtually ubiquitous in rough grassland throughout central and southern Europe, but absent from much of the north.

■ *confirmed range*

ESSEX SKIPPER *Thymelicus lineola*

Adult identification
Average wingspan 27 mm (♂) to 30 mm (♀)

The wing markings in both sexes are almost identical, with the male scent mark no more than a fine black line across his upper forewing. The ground colour is

▲ The female of this mating pair of Essex Skippers has her wings open, whilst the male shows the black tips of his antennae that distinguish Essex from Small Skippers.

orange-brown on the upperwings, with faint black veins and black wing margins. The underwings are dull orange tinged with grey-green, and are plain.

Essex and Small Skippers are indistinguishable in flight and similar at rest: see pages 29 and 48 for distinguishing features. These two Skippers fly together on many sites, the Essex emerging one to two weeks later, but with a considerable overlap. Unless egg-laying is seen, it will be necessary to examine the tips of the antennae.

Young stages
A short row of smooth milk-white **eggs** is laid within firm flower sheaths on coarse grasses. Each is flat, like that of the Small Skipper, but more oval in outline. It also differs from the latter species by hibernating as an egg.

Like the Small and Lulworth Skipper, the **caterpillar** lives mainly in a folded

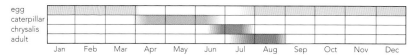

	Jan	Feb	Mar	Apr	May	Jun	Jul	Aug	Sep	Oct	Nov	Dec
egg												
caterpillar												
chrysalis												
adult												

blade of grass, fastened by stout silk cords to form a tube. It feeds on a wide range of coarse grasses (see Habitat). The fully grown caterpillar is pale green, striped with dark green down the back and yellow along the sides. The head differs from the Small Skipper's in being striped with pale brown.

The **chrysalis** occurs in a coarse netlike tent of silk spun between folded grass blades. It is yellow-green, and the beak is white, not pink as in the Small Skipper.

Habitat and behaviour

Like all our 'golden' Skippers, the Essex flies and breeds in self-contained colonies and is rather easy to overlook. Colonies should be sought in rough, tall grassland, including isolated strips such as hedgerows, road verges and the rides and edges of woods. Vast numbers occur on some abandoned or lightly grazed chalk grassland, but it is also common on some acid soils, as well as among the wetlands and salt marshes of East Anglia, where it was originally discovered. The range of coarse grasses eaten by the caterpillar is unknown, but cocksfoot (*Dactylis glomerata*) and creeping soft grass (*Holcus mollis*) are the main species, with timothy (*Phleum pratense*) probably important in some habitats. Caterpillars are occasionally found also on wood false brome (*Brachypodium sylvaticum*) and tor grass (*B. pinnatum*), but not on Yorkshire fog, the foodplant of the Small Skipper. Breeding everywhere is confined to tall mature clumps of these grasses.

The adults spend long periods at rest, perched on warm patches of bare ground or amongst dense vegetation. In full sunshine they make short, rapid skipping flights, at grasshead height buzzing from flower to flower.

Distribution and status

The Essex Skipper is confined to England, south of the Humber. Colonies – some huge – are common in rough grassland and salt marshes throughout East Anglia, Kent, Surrey, Sussex, Hampshire, Wiltshire, Lincolnshire and the East Midlands. Its status elsewhere is poorly known because few naturalists bother to check small Skippers in western and northern counties. It is always worth doing so, and repeating checks in the future, for this is a butterfly that has rapidly expanded in range over the past 35 years. At present, it remains locally distributed throughout Dorset, and scattered colonies occur in Cornwall, Devon, Somerset and the Cotswolds. It has already crossed the border into Wales, and recently colonized south-east Ireland.

In Europe, the Essex Skipper is common in central and southern regions, and occurs over a wider range than the Small Skipper, for example in Sweden.

confirmed range

LULWORTH SKIPPER *Thymelicus acteon*

Adult identification

Average wingspan 25 mm (♂) to 27 mm (♀)

The smallest and darkest of the 'golden' Skippers, the upperwings are dun or olive-brown, dusted with gold, with black margins. The female is lighter and has a distinct circle of gold rays on the upperside of each forewing (like the eye of a peacock's feather), which reflects the sun. This pattern is faintly visible on

▲ A female Lulworth Skipper feeding on the Isle of Purbeck on the Dorset coast. Note the golden 'peacock eye' on the upper forewing which shines in the sunlight.

some males (page 29), which also have a black scent bar across each forewing. The underwings of both male and female are uniformly straw-coloured.

The female Lulworth Skipper is distinguished from Large and Silver-spotted Skippers by the 'peacock's feather' of gold marks, its much smaller size, and plain underwings. The male is smaller and darker than the Small or Essex Skipper and the undersurface of each antenna is cream-coloured.

Young stages

Up to 15, but usually five or six, pale yellow oval **eggs** are laid in a row in the flower sheaths of tor grass, especially in dead brown growth. Look for them in August when they are quite easy to find.

The **caterpillars** hibernate without feeding, in a row of tiny white cocoons spun where the eggs were laid. They disperse in April to live alone in tubes of folded tor grass blades fastened double by silk. At dusk each caterpillar eats the blade above and, eventually, below it,

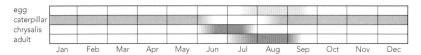

	Jan	Feb	Mar	Apr	May	Jun	Jul	Aug	Sep	Oct	Nov	Dec
egg												
caterpillar												
chrysalis												
adult												

making distinctive V-shaped notches and later leaving the tube isolated on the midrib. This is very easy to find in June. The caterpillar is up to 25 mm long, pale green with dark green and cream stripes. That of the Essex Skipper has brown stripes on its head, whilst the Small Skipper caterpillar is dark green down its back.

The **chrysalis** is hard to find in a loose cocoon of grass and silk near the ground. It is about 17 mm long, with pale green head and wings, bright green thorax, and yellow-green abdomen. The beak on the head is twice as long as that of the Small Skipper.

Habitat and behaviour

This is a butterfly of warm south-facing rough hillsides, clifftops, and undercliffs. It is restricted to base-rich soils near the south coast, where tor grass (*Brachypodium pinnatum*) is abundant. However, breeding occurs only where this coarse grass grows both in dense mature clumps, at least 20 cm tall, and in sunny sheltered spots. Most broken undercliffs and some abandoned hillsides in south-east Dorset contain acres of this habitat, where the Lulworth Skipper still flies in prodigious numbers on a few sites, the adults jostling for nectar on marjoram, thistles and other flowers right down to the shoreline. Much smaller colonies inhabit the grazed and exposed hillsides in this region, breeding in scattered patches where tall clumps of tor grass grow in sheltered spots beside stone walls, amongst scrub, or in abandoned pits. Flights are brief, rapid and buzzing, like all the 'golden' Skippers.

Distribution and status

About 75 British colonies of the Lulworth Skipper exist; all are in Dorset where it breeds along the coast between Swanage and Weymouth on all chalk and limestone cliffs and undercliffs. There is another string of colonies 1–5 miles inland, running parallel to the coast along the steep south-facing chalk escarpment of the Purbeck Hills. Many inland colonies are small, but on abandoned hillsides and on the undercliffs a few populations of several hundred thousand adults occur. It is especially abundant east and west of Lulworth Cove, after which it was named. Elsewhere, a few small colonies exist at Burton Bradstock, and it recently colonized Portland, but the old Devon colonies are extinct.

This little Skipper increased enormously in the second half of the 20th century in Dorset, having benefited from the lack of grazing by rabbits following myxomatosis and the subsequent invasion of coarse grasses. More recently, several colonies have been lost with the return of rabbits and others have declined, but many survive and are internationally important, for this is a rapidly declining butterfly over most of its central and north European range.

▦ confirmed range

SILVER-SPOTTED SKIPPER *Hesperia comma*

Adult identification

Average wingspan 30 mm (♂) to 36 mm (♀)

The underwings are the most distinctive feature of both sexes, and give this Skipper its name: they are olive-green and marked with conspicuous silver patches. The upperwings have gold or yellow marks on a dark brown back-

▲ *The beautiful Silver-spotted Skipper was named after the silver spots on its greenish underwings. It is rare, but recovering after being close to extinction in the 1970s.*

ground. The contrast is greater in the female, which has brighter marks and a deeper ground colour. The male is much smaller and has a black bar of scent scales across each upper forewing.

Old faded Large Skippers (page 56) can survive to September and are often mistaken for this butterfly. In flight they are nearly identical, although young Large Skippers are more golden. At rest, the undersurfaces appear very different, with only a faint ginger and gold pattern and no silver on the Large Skipper. No other Skipper on the continent closely resembles either of these species, but see the female Lulworth Skipper which, although tiny, has somewhat similar upperwings (page 52).

Young stages

The **egg**, laid singly, is quite large (about 0.7 mm high) and is easy to find if suitable sheep's fescue (see Habitat) is examined in late summer or autumn. It is yellow-white, smooth and shaped like a tiny

	Jan	Feb	Mar	Apr	May	Jun	Jul	Aug	Sep	Oct	Nov	Dec

egg
caterpillar
chrysalis
adult

pudding-basin placed upside down on the side of a leaf blade.

The **caterpillar** is difficult but not impossible to find, living solitarily in a small tent of sheep's fescue leaves spun together by silk. It has an olive-green, wrinkled grub-like body, up to 25 mm long, with a black head.

The **chrysalis** is formed in a tough cocoon at the base of grass stems and is even harder to find than the caterpillar. It is pale olive-brown with much darker head, thorax and wing cases, and the whole surface is covered with short bristles.

Habitat and behaviour

This is a sun-loving butterfly that is restricted to the hottest parts of Britain. It occurs in discrete colonies, mainly on the steep, thin-soiled, south-facing slopes of southern chalk downs. The caterpillars feed solely on sheep's fescue (*Festuca ovina*). This fine-leaved grass is still abundant on many unfertilized downs, but only certain plants are acceptable: egg-laying is largely confined to small isolated tufts growing beside bare ground, especially in sunny depressions such as hoofprints. In warm years, they are slightly less particular. The size of a colony is directly related to the amount of suitable sheep's fescue present. Today, many warm downs are too overgrown to support colonies of this Skipper, whilst on marginal sites, breeding is confined to a few sparse 'islands', such as path edges. Good sites, with thousands of adults, contain several acres of short sheep's fescue growing very sparsely amongst crumbly chalk scree.

The adults tend to be inconspicuous even on the best sites because they are inactive unless the air temperature exceeds 20°C, and even then spend long periods out of sight, basking in pockets of bare ground. Flight is short and rapid, buzzing just above the close-cropped turf between a wide range of chalk flowers.

Distribution and status

This is one of our rarest butterflies. Colonies once bred on many base-rich hillsides up to Yorkshire, but apart from one limestone site in Somerset, they are now restricted to a few isolated areas of chalk, mainly on steep escarpments in the south Chilterns, north Dorset, Hampshire, south Sussex, and on the North Downs between Guildford and Reigate and in south-east Kent. Many colonies disappeared following the collapse of rabbit grazing due to myxomatosis in the 1950s to 1970s, but, with targeted conservation and the partial return of rabbits coinciding with a run of warm summers, many former sites have been reoccupied. There are now at least 250 colonies, a three- to four-fold increase since the 1970s. The best contain several thousand adults.

▦ *confirmed range*

LARGE SKIPPER *Ochlodes venata*

Adult identification

Average wingspan 33 mm (♂) to 35 mm (♀)

A sturdy Skipper with long antennae, distinctly clubbed at the tips. The upperwings are brown around the edges with large bright orange patches towards the

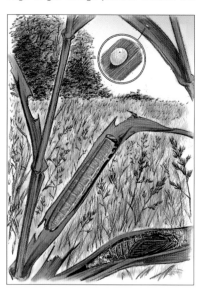

▲ *The male Large Skipper perches alone with his wings held apart waiting for passing females. It is a common butterfly throughout the lowlands of England and Wales.*

body, divided by black veins. This pattern is clearer in the female, whilst the male has a large black scent line across the middle of each upper forewing. The underwings are duller in both sexes, with a faint pattern of orange patches against a greenish-brown background. This is the only common Skipper with orange and brown patterned wings. The rare Silver-spotted Skipper has similar upperwings but distinct silver patches on the underwings (page 54); the female Lulworth Skipper (page 52), though much smaller, is superficially similar. No additional continental species resembles these three, but note that the Silver-spotted Skipper is as common as the Large Skipper in central Europe.

Young stages

The **egg** is dome-shaped in profile, circular from above, and quite large (0.8 mm high). It is pearl white, and is laid singly under the

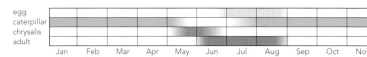

	Jan	Feb	Mar	Apr	May	Jun	Jul	Aug	Sep	Oct	Nov	Dec
egg												
caterpillar												
chrysalis												
adult												

leaf blades of cocksfoot or, sometimes, wood false brome. It is not easy to find.

The **caterpillar** feeds on grass, living in a blade held double by little ropes of silk to form a tube, or sitting exposed on a leaf when fully grown. It hibernates, half grown, in a sturdier tent of several leaf blades, and resumes feeding in spring. Fairly easy to find, the caterpillar is blue-green when fully grown, with a dark green line down the centre and a cream-coloured line along each side. The head is dark.

The **chrysalis** is very dark, especially on the head, thorax and wing cases, with a waxy bloom. Search for it in its silk and grass blade tent in early June.

Habitat and behaviour

The Large Skipper lives in distinct colonies in a wide range of rough places where wild grasses grow unchecked. The usual foodplant is cocksfoot (*Dactylis glomerata*), although wood false brome (*Brachypodium sylvaticum*) is sometimes used and can possibly support a colony. In either case, tall clumps growing in sunny sheltered positions are used for breeding. Look for colonies in un-improved grassland, along hedgerows and road verges and, especially, on the edges, rides and glades of woods and in rough scrubby places: it prefers more sheltered sites than the Essex or Small Skipper, although all three are often found together.

The adults fly only in sunshine and, like most Skippers, appear to buzz and skip above the grassheads. They frequently land on shrubs, especially the males which establish individual perching posts on prominent leaves in sunny corners, from where each sorties after passing females in rapid swirling flights. Between flights he will usually return to the same leaf, and can then be closely observed.

Distribution and status

The Large Skipper is absent from Ireland and, despite a recent northwards expansion, it remains a scarce butterfly in Scotland, confined only to the south-west. Farther south the Large Skipper is absent at high altitudes in the Lake District, Pennines, and Welsh mountains, but is otherwise one of the commonest species throughout all lowland areas of England and Wales. There can be little doubt that numerous lowland colonies have disappeared in recent decades, due to the intensification of agriculture, the shadiness of modern forestry plantations, and the general tidying up of the countryside; nevertheless, colonies are still to be expected wherever extensive clumps of cocksfoot and tall wild grasses occur.

The Large Skipper is also very common throughout much of Europe, extending well into Norway and Sweden. It is absent, however, from southern Spain.

▧ confirmed range

DINGY SKIPPER *Erynnis tages*

Adult identification

Average wingspan 29 mm

Both sexes of this moth-like Skipper look much the same. The upperwings are mainly grey-brown, with a blurred pattern on the forewings of darker patches and shiny areas, and an oily-looking sheen in sunshine. Tiny white dots embellish the outer edges of all wings and the fringes are pale grey. There is some variation in the strength of this

▲ *The Dingy Skipper emerges in spring and is the most moth-like of all the butterflies found in the British Isles.*

pattern, and old adults look truly dingy and very pale. The underwings are light grey-brown, unmarked except for small white dots. Although it is easy to identify in Britain, beginners sometimes confuse Dingy and Grizzled Skippers (page 60): the latter has a much more contrasting pattern, especially on the underwings, and distinctly chequered black and white fringes.

Young stages

The **egg** is dome-shaped in profile, round from above, and has several distinct ribs running from the summit to the base. Although pale when laid, it soon turns bright orange and is easy to find on bird's-foot trefoil, greater bird's-foot trefoil, or horseshoe vetch. Search on the upper surfaces in the groove where the leaves join the stem, or on the tenderest young leaflets.

The **caterpillar** feeds on vetch leaves and lives alone in a loose tent of its foodplant spun near the ground. It can be found, with practice, in midsummer; the caterpillar is then fully grown and uniformly green with a purplish-black

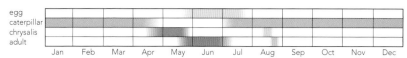

	Jan	Feb	Mar	Apr	May	Jun	Jul	Aug	Sep	Oct	Nov	Dec
egg												
caterpillar												
chrysalis												
adult												

head. It hibernates in a more substantial tent from late July onwards.

The **chrysalis** is formed in the hibernation tent in spring. The dark green thorax and wing cases contrast with a warm chestnut-coloured abdomen.

Habitat and behaviour

Nearly all colonies of Dingy Skipper breed on bird's-foot trefoil (*Lotus corniculatus*) and are found where this vetch grows in abundance in sunny sheltered places. The best sites are dunes and rough ground round the coast, and ancient chalk and limestone downs where the turf is open or fairly short; horseshoe vetch (*Hippocrepis comosa*) is also eaten on these latter sites. Smaller colonies occur also on heaths, embankments, wasteland, and disturbed or rough ground that is not too overgrown to suppress the foodplant. In woods, there may be small numbers along the broad mown rides of modern plantations, in areas of young coppice, or in damper glades where greater bird's-foot trefoil (*L. uliginosus*) grows.

This butterfly lives in small self-contained colonies which typically contain tens rather than hundreds of adults. The males congregate in sheltered hollows or at the base of hills and, on sunny days, both sexes spend long periods basking on patches of bare ground, with the wings held wide apart, pressed against the warm soil. Flight is swift, whirring just above the ground. At night and in cool weather, they perch on dead flowers or grassheads around which they drape their wings, looking very like moths.

Distribution and status

Apart from the newly discovered Essex Skipper, this is the only Skipper to be found in Ireland, where it is widely but very locally distributed and is frequent only in the Burren; curiously, it is absent from most of the Irish coastline. In Scotland, a few colonies breed in the north-east (much further north than other Skippers) and there are more along the south-west coast. The coastline of England and Wales also supports a string of colonies which, although not occurring continuously, may be encountered almost anywhere except along flat muddy stretches such as around the Wash. Inland colonies are much more localized in England and Wales. They occur most frequently on downs and in woods in southern counties and become scarce north of the Chilterns and the Cotswolds. Colonies are absent from high altitudes.

In short this is our most widely distributed Skipper, although nowhere is it anything like so common as Large, Essex or Small Skippers are in the south. This was not always true of some southern counties, but countless inland colonies of Dingy Skipper have recently been lost due to intensive agriculture and forestry, a trend that shows little sign of abatement.

▓▓▓ *confirmed range*

GRIZZLED SKIPPER *Pyrgus malvae*

Adult identification

Average wingspan 27 mm

Both sexes look much the same and are best distinguished by the shorter stumpier body of the female. On the

▲ *A Grizzled Skipper basks with its wings wide open in the sunshine. When in flight the chequered wings blur, making it hard to follow.*

uppersides, the wings are a chequer-board of black and white markings and the fringes have conspicuous black and white bars. The undersides are similar, but duller, and the hindwing has large white marks on a greenish background (page 29). It is unlikely that any other British butterfly will be confused with this species except, possibly, the Dingy Skipper (pages 29 and 58). Certain day-flying moths look similar in flight, and on the continent, there are 19 other extremely similar Skippers which can be identified only by netting and reference to a European guide.

Young stages

The **egg** is pale green, fading to white, and dome-shaped with about 20 ribs running from the summit to the base. About 0.5 mm tall, it is laid on the underside, and occasionally upperside, of a small

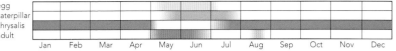

	Jan	Feb	Mar	Apr	May	Jun	Jul	Aug	Sep	Oct	Nov	Dec
egg												
caterpillar												
chrysalis												
adult												

leaf of its foodplant (see Habitat), and is possible but not easy to find.

In July, the tiny yellow **caterpillar** rests under fine silk along the midrib of the upperside of the leaf, leaving blotches on the leaf where it has fed; it is quite easy to find. When older, it has a dark green body with brown stripes (much darker than the Dingy Skipper caterpillar) and a black head. It lives in a loose tent formed by drawing the edges of a leaf around itself.

The **chrysalis** is chestnut-brown with contrasting white wing cases. It occurs in a loose cocoon of neat silk netting spun near the base of its foodplant. It may be found from autumn onwards.

Habitat and behaviour

The caterpillars feed on the leaves of several members of the rose family, usually wild strawberry (*Fragaria vesca*), creeping cinquefoil (*Potentilla repens*) or agrimony (*Agrimonia eupatotia*), with tormentil and blackberry (short, stumpy bushes only) less often used. It lives in small discrete colonies which seldom consist of more than a hundred adults. These are found where their foodplants grow in sunny sheltered places, usually among sparse, but not necessarily very short vegetation. Typical sites are recent clearings, broad rides and the edges of woods; rough sheltered grassland among scrub, especially on chalk and limestone downs; and any warm crumbling bank.

The adult is an active little butterfly with a darting flight that is hard to follow due to the blurred effect of the chequered wings. However, it frequently alights, often on bare ground, and may be closely approached as it sits basking with its back towards the sun. As with the Dingy Skipper, a few adults occasionally emerge to form a partial second brood during August.

Distribution and status

Like the Dingy Skipper, with which it often flies, numerous inland colonies of the Grizzled Skipper have disappeared in recent years due to the increased shadiness of woods, the intensification of agriculture, and the tidying up of the countryside. Moreover, its foodplants are much less common along the undisturbed coast than the Dingy Skipper, being mainly confined to cliffs and undercliffs. Today, the Grizzled Skipper is local, and alas declining, in central southern counties of England, and is distinctly scarce both in the south-west and north of the Cotswolds and Chilterns. In the Midlands and East Anglia it is now mainly confined to a few larger woods, and it may now be extinct on former sites north of the Wash. It is absent from Ireland, extinct in Scotland, and very rare in Wales apart from a few scattered colonies on scrubby cliffs along the coast.

confirmed range

SWALLOWTAIL *Papilio machaon*

Adult identification

Average wingspan 80 mm (♂) to 90 mm (♀)

Both sexes of this very large and unmistakable butterfly are similar. Note the long tails below a blue border con-

young caterpillar

▲ *The Swallowtail, the British Isles' most spectacular butterfly, perching on milk parsley in the Norfolk Broads.*

taining an orange eye, and the bold black and pale yellow markings of the wings. These, however, blur into the colour of weak tea when the Swallowtail is in flight. No other British butterfly is remotely similar. The British Swallowtail belongs to a subspecies that is unique to this country. Continental Swallowtails are paler, with thinner black borders and veins. There is also another continental species, the even larger Scarce Swallowtail, which is not scarce at all and has vertical black stripes on a paler background.

Young stages

The globular **egg** is pale yellow at first, but turns brown after a few days. It is laid singly on the caterpillar's foodplant, milk parsley, and is quite easy to find. Search the forked leaves of prominent plants in the Norfolk Broads in June.

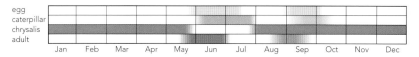

	Jan	Feb	Mar	Apr	May	Jun	Jul	Aug	Sep	Oct	Nov	Dec
egg												
caterpillar												
chrysalis												
adult												

The **caterpillar** too can be found by searching suitable milk parsley in summer. At first it looks like a small bird dropping: black and spiny with a white band. When older it is smooth and plump, beautifully striped with black on a fleshy-green background. It has an unusual way of deterring enemies: a large orange horn (the osmeterium) is extruded from a fold behind the head, and gives off an unpleasant smell.

The colour of the **chrysalis** varies from green to pale grey with black marks. It is hard to find on reed stems or its foodplant. A few hatch to form a partial second brood of adults each summer, but the majority hibernate.

Habitat and behaviour

The British subspecies of the Swallowtail requires extensive areas of wetlands and fens, and is now confined to the Norfolk Broads. The caterpillar's only foodplant is milk parsley (*Peucedanum palustre*). Robust, tall, flowering specimens are selected for egg-laying, and these grow only in the wettest marshes, especially where the reedbeds are kept open by regular cutting. In many places, the Broads were becoming too dry and overgrown for this butterfly, but optimum conditions are now maintained on nature reserves, and indeed more widely throughout the Broads.

The Swallowtail is a magnificent insect, with a powerful gliding flight, and can still be seen quite regularly over the open water as it flies from one reedbed to the next.

The paler continental subspecies of the Swallowtail is much more mobile and breeds on a range of umbellifers in other habitats. It occasionally reaches southern counties and establishes itself for a year or two on chalk downs breeding mainly on the wild carrot (*Daucus carota*).

Distribution and status

Colonies of the British Swallowtail once bred throughout the fenlands of Cambridgeshire and east Lincolnshire, and in other wetlands in the south, but all were destroyed when these areas were drained. The last fenland colony survived until the 1950s on a nature reserve at Wicken, near Cambridge, but even this became unsuitable as neighbouring land was drained. The Swallowtail is now confined to the Norfolk Broads, where it is still quite widespread. It is locally numerous, and still easy to see in early June, on suitable marshes around the rivers Ant, Thurne, Bure and mid-Yare. Occasional single individuals may also be seen elsewhere in Britain, mainly near butterfly farms from which they periodically escape. Migrants from the continent are very rarely encountered on southern chalk downs, mostly in Kent and Dorset.

▓▓▓ confirmed range

63

WOOD WHITE *Leptidea sinapis*

Adult identification

Average wingspan 42 mm

This is our smallest White and, until the Cryptic Wood White was recently discovered in Ireland, one of the easiest to identify (see pages 30 and 66–67 for the small differences between the two

▲ *This female Wood White is curving her abdomen to lay a minute egg on a vetch leaflet. The caterpillar feeds on the vetch leaves and is easily spotted when fully grown in July.*

Wood Whites). When settled, the wings of Wood Whites are never opened, so only the undersides are seen. These are long, thin and oval – quite unlike the rounded shape of other Whites. The ground colour is yellow-white, with darker patches, but no real pattern, of grey-green scales. The dainty flight of this butterfly is idiosyncratic: the wings are flapped so slowly that you can clearly see black tips to the male's upper forewings. On females, these tip markings are absent or just a faint dusting of grey scales. During spring, inexperienced butterfly watchers often mistake small, weak-flying male Green-veined Whites for this scarce butterfly: the differences are obvious when they settle.

Young stages

The **egg** is bottle-shaped, off-white, and somewhat glassy in appearance. It is laid on the undersurfaces of vetch leaves, on

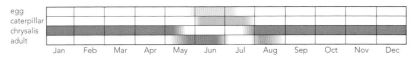

	Jan	Feb	Mar	Apr	May	Jun	Jul	Aug	Sep	Oct	Nov	Dec
egg												
caterpillar												
chrysalis												
adult												

plants growing proud above the surrounding vegetation in sunny sheltered spots, and can be found quite easily by searching the youngest leaflets in June.

The **caterpillar** feeds on vetch leaves and is possible to find when fully grown in July. It is tubular in shape and pale green, with a darker green stripe running down its back and a yellow stripe along each side.

The pretty pointed **chrysalis** is green with pink streaks, but is almost impossible to find among the dense vegetation in which it hibernates.

Habitat and behaviour

This delicate little butterfly rarely strays from its discrete colonies. These are few and far between, but on good sites may contain thousands of adults. Search where there is an abundance of the caterpillar's foodplants – meadow vetchling (*Lathyrus pratensis*), bitter vetch (*L. montanus*), tufted vetch (*Vicia cracca*) and bird's-foot trefoil (*Lotus corniculatus*) – growing as tall bushy plants that project above other vegetation in sunny sheltered places. Typical sites are recently cleared woods that are beginning to grow up again, ditches and scrubby edges to broad sunny rides in young plantations, scrubby broken undercliffs, abandoned railway cuttings and, in west Ireland, warm limestone pavement sheltered by hazel scrub.

Whatever the habitat, the males are conspicuous as they flap and flutter almost in slow motion, sometimes hovering a foot or two above the ground, at other times patrolling rides and clearings in a systematic quest for a female. She flies less often but, when seen, is just as weak and delicate as the male. In warm years there is a partial second brood of adults in summer, but essentially this is a springtime butterfly.

Distribution and status

The Wood White is a scarce insect in England and Wales, now reduced to around 90 sites. Colonies occur, very locally, in plantations and railway cuttings in the southern English Midlands, the Wye Valley, east Wales, and Devon, especially on the coast. A few breed in the west Weald of Surrey and Sussex, and one or two in Hampshire, Dorset, Wiltshire and Somerset. This butterfly was much commoner in the 19th century, but declined drastically after coppicing was abandoned in most woodlands. There has been a small recovery in young plantations in recent years, often helped by deliberate reintroductions, while conservation management has produced a welcome increase on several nature reserves. In Ireland, *L. sinapis* is as localized as in Britain. It has been positively identified only on the eastern side of the Burren (Co. Clare) and in similar sheltered limestone pavement in south-east Galway.

■■■ confirmed range

CRYPTIC WOOD WHITE *Leptidea juvernica*

Adult identification

Average wingspan 42 mm

In 2011, the Cryptic Wood White (*Leptidea juvernica*) was identified as a separate species from Réal's Wood White (*L. reali*), which had itself been identified on the continent as a distinct species

▲ The Cryptic Wood White is the commonest species of Wood White in Ireland, but so far the species has never been found in England, Wales or Scotland.

from *L. sinapis* as recently as 1988. The adults of both our species are too similar to distinguish from wing pattern, although in Sweden the second generation of female *L. juvernica* has a dusky patch on the tip of each upper forewing whereas in *L. sinapis* these are white. This is a less helpful character in Britain, where a second generation of *L. juvernica* is virtually unknown (except when bred in captivity). Friburg and Wiklund also found that the patch of white scales beneath the tip of the antenna was bolder in male *L. sinapis*, although these drop off with age making the distinction imprecise for older males. Finally, courtship differs: the males of both species stand head on to a resting female, waving the white-tipped antennae and uncurled proboscis in her face for 30 minutes, but male *L. sinapis* also flap their wings a couple of times every 30 seconds or so; male *L. juvernica* never do.

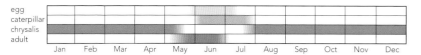

	Jan	Feb	Mar	Apr	May	Jun	Jul	Aug	Sep	Oct	Nov	Dec
egg												
caterpillar												
chrysalis												
adult												

On current knowledge, the surest way to distinguish between our two Wood Whites is to examine genitalia preparations from dead adults through a microscope, a technique familiar to all who identify moths. When females are compared (see page 30), the ductus bursae is distinctly shorter in *L. sinapis* (0.59–0.70 mm) than in *L. juvernica* (0.86–1.11 mm). Male differences are less clear-cut, but the aedeagus and saccus are also shorter in *L. sinapis*. Nelson and Hughes examined many British 'Wood Whites' in this way, and found only *L. sinapis* in England and Wales, and in a discrete area in west Ireland, where *L. juvernica* is absent. In contrast, *L. juvernica* was the only Wood White found in the rest of Ireland. Thus on present knowledge, the location of a colony provides a reasonable distinction between these sister species.

Young stages

The **egg** and **caterpillar** of the Cryptic Wood White are identical to those of the Wood White, and found in the same positions on the same foodplants. The **chrysalis** differs, at least in Sweden. Friburg found that in *L. sinapis* the sheath covering the antenna is white with a clean red stripe running down the middle, especially near the antennal club, whereas in the Cryptic Wood White the red is diffuse and mingles with the white pigment.

Habitat and behaviour

In Ireland, the Cryptic Wood White inhabits short to mid-height flower-rich grassland, especially where there are scattered shrubs or other shelter. Colonies occur on coastal dunes, unimproved meadows, fen edges and cut-over bogs, and along tracks and rides in woods. Others breed on man-made sites, including disused quarries and along railway and road verges. The main foodplants in all these habitats are yellow vetchling (*Lathyrus pratensis* – for which it has a greater penchant than even *L. sinapis*), bird's-foot trefoil (*Lotus corniculatus*) and probably bitter and tufted vetches.

Distribution and status

The Cryptic Wood White has never been found in England or Wales despite thorough examinations of genitalia. But in Ireland, every specimen examined was a Cryptic Wood White, apart from in the Burren and just north in County Galway, where only *L. sinapis* occurs: there appears to be no overlap between the two species. Recent surveys confirm that the Cryptic Wood White is a widespread and locally common species across most of Ireland. Although many colonies have recently been lost due to the intensification of agriculture and road verge management, it has expanded northwards and in south-west Ireland.

▨ possible
   distribution

▨ confirmed
   range

CLOUDED YELLOW *Colias croceus*

Adult identification

Average wingspan 57 mm (♂) to 62 mm (♀)

When settled, the Clouded Yellow

▲ *The Clouded Yellow with its yellow wings and silver 'figure of eight' in the centre forming an attractive contrast to its green eyes and pink legs.*

hardly ever opens its wings so normally only the underwings are seen. These are deep yellow, with a black spot halfway across the forewing. In the centre of each hindwing is a pair of silver spots surrounded by reddish-brown forming a conspicuous figure of '8'. Yellow-green eyes peer out from a yellow head and body. The butterfly is usually seen in rapid flight, thus revealing rich orange upperwings with broad black borders that cannot be confused with any other species. There is, however, a pale form of the female, called *helice*, in which the orange ground colour is replaced by grey: it is quite common in some years, comprising up to 10% of females, and looks identical, in flight, to the Pale Clouded Yellow and Berger's Clouded

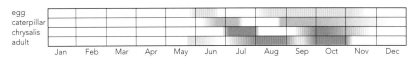

	Jan	Feb	Mar	Apr	May	Jun	Jul	Aug	Sep	Oct	Nov	Dec
egg												
caterpillar												
chrysalis												
adult												

Yellow (page 167), which are always much rarer than *helice*. Note that the black border on *helice* is darker and broader on the hindwing and extends further round the lower edge of the forewing (page 32).

Young stages

The **egg** is bottle-shaped and pale yellow when laid, but turns pink then orange after a day or two. It is laid singly, usually in mid-June, often on the uppersides of legume (clover, lucerne and trefoil) leaves, and is not too difficult to find in 'Clouded Yellow Years'.

The **caterpillar** is very hard to spot among its leguminous foodplants. It feeds on the leaves and, when fully grown, is dark green with a yellow line along each side with orange circles round the spiracles.

The **chrysalis** is pale yellow-green, but is well hidden and unlikely to be found.

Habitat and behaviour

The Clouded Yellow is a migratory butterfly that is unable to survive British winters, apart from the very mildest and then only in insignificant numbers. Winter breeding occurs round the Mediterranean. Each spring the offspring fly north through Europe, to reach Britain's southern shores in highly variable numbers every year. These spread northwards in diminishing numbers, occasionally reaching Scotland. Flight is powerful and rapid, but they also linger awhile when breeding sites are encountered. These can be cultivated fields sown with clovers or alfalfa, whilst unsprayed flowery downland, with an abundance of trefoils or vetches, is also a favourite habitat. In addition to these concentrations, roaming adults may be seen, usually singly, in any other habitat, including gardens.

Distribution and status

The distribution and abundance of the Clouded Yellow varies enormously from one year to the next, depending largely on how many immigrants arrive in spring. In some years there are very few, but normally one expects to see this butterfly in ones and twos on southern downs and coastal grasslands in high summer. Sometimes there is a large immigration, which breeds up to produce extraordinary numbers in the second and subsequent broods. The butterfly is then a common sight throughout the countryside of southern England, Wales and Ireland, whilst smaller numbers penetrate into northern England and even Scotland. These 'Clouded Yellow Years' were once few and far between – and included a 35-year gap prior to 1983 – but have occurred more frequently during recent warm seasons, with seven examples during the past 20 years.

Immigrants are occasionally seen from April to early June. The second brood from mid-July onwards is much larger.

██ maximum
range

BRIMSTONE *Gonepteryx rhamni*

Adult identification

Average wingspan 60 mm

The Brimstone is a fairly large butterfly

▲ *The Brimstone has distinctive pink antennae. Perching with its wings closed, as here, it has a marvellous leaf-like camouflage.*

and one of the easiest to identify. The male has clear yellow wings which, in flight, can be mistaken only for the Clouded Yellow. The latter is smaller, darker, and a deeper orange-yellow. The female Brimstone has much paler upper wings compared to the male, with a green tint that, at a distance, can easily be misidentified for a Large White (page 31). Both sexes are unmistakable at rest. They always sit with their wings closed, so only the undersides are seen. These look extraordinarily like a pale yellow leaf, with pointed corners, prominent veins, and even a spot of 'mould' in the centre. The body and legs are the same pale yellow, but the eyes are large, black and shiny. Note, too, the beautiful clubbed antennae which sprout from between the eyes like a pair of pink stalks.

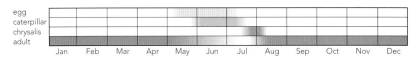

	Jan	Feb	Mar	Apr	May	Jun	Jul	Aug	Sep	Oct	Nov	Dec
egg												
caterpillar												
chrysalis												
adult												

Young stages

The **egg** is off-white and bottle-shaped. It is very easy to find in late spring, singly, on purging buckthorn and alder buckthorn bushes. Search beneath the tenderest young leafshoots on the tips of branches growing in sunny sheltered situations.

The **caterpillar** is just as easy to spot and at all ages, for it sits exposed along the midrib of a leaf, leaving obvious feeding damage on the leaves around it. It is tubular with a white stripe and bluish-green tinge that blends well with the colour of its background.

The **chrysalis** is fleshy green with purple marks and curiously leaf-like. It is usually formed on nearby vegetation, and very hard, but not impossible, to find.

Habitat and behaviour

The Brimstone is a conspicuous butterfly of woods, hedgerows and scrubby places. The adults emerge in August, and immediately prepare for hibernation by gorging themselves on nectar, some-times continuing well into November. They do not live in compact colonies, but wander through the countryside, often entering gardens to feed. Although usually seen in ones or twos, scores sometimes gather on teasels and thistles along woodland rides in late summer. Hibernation occurs mainly in woods, deep among evergreens such as holly and ivy.

The adults re-emerge on the first warm days of spring and again roam, this time in search of mates and egg-laying sites. Females have an extraordinary ability to find even the most isolated of buckthorn bushes; purging buckthorn (*Rhamnus cathartica*) and alder buckthorn (*Frangula alnus*) are equally acceptable. Both grow in scrub, along wood edges and rides, and less often, in hedges. Brimstones are sure to be found wherever these food-plants are common.

Distribution and status

The Brimstone's range coincides almost exactly with that of its two foodplants. It is common through most of southern England up to Humberside, breeding on purging buckthorn on calcareous and neutral soils, and on alder buckthorn in wetter, peaty or acidic areas. Although there has been a considerable expansion in the north of its range, its most northern sites remain in the Lake District, although strays reach Scotland. In Wales it is a very local species, except in the south-east and the border counties. Although peat bogs abound in Ireland, alder buckthorn is rare, hence the Brimstone is mainly found in the limestone areas breeding on purging buckthorn. It is, however, a reasonably common butterfly around the Burren and in central counties.

▓▓▓▓ confirmed range

LARGE WHITE *Pieris brassicae*

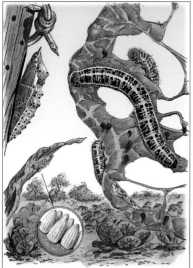

▲ *The male Large White has neat black tips to his forewings but lacks the wing-spots found on females.*

Adult identification

Average wingspan 63 mm (♂) to 70 mm (♀)

The upperwings of this large butterfly are gleaming white, with conspicuous black tips to the forewings. The female also has a pair of black spots in the middle of each forewing and a black smear along the lower edge (page 31). These marks are slightly greyer in the spring brood. The underwings are pale yellow dusted with grey, and have no pattern.

Size alone distinguishes the Large White from our other white butterflies, but note that the female Brimstone looks similar in flight (page 70). The occasional

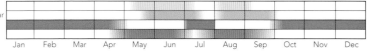

| | Jan | Feb | Mar | Apr | May | Jun | Jul | Aug | Sep | Oct | Nov | Dec |

small individual may be distinguished from the Green-veined White and female Orange Tip by its unpatterned underwings, whilst the dark tip on the upper forewing of the Small White is confined to the extreme tip, and does not extend down the outer edge (page 74). In addition, the male Small White has a black spot in the centre of the forewing.

Young stages

The **eggs** are yellow, bottle-shaped and laid in neat groups of 50–100 on the leaves of cabbages and other foodplants, usually on the undersides. They are easy to find.

The **caterpillars**, too, are extremely conspicuous. At first pale green, they turn a mottled grey-green when fully grown with black splodges and short white hairs, and smell most unpleasant. They live gregariously exposed on brassica plants, which can be stripped to a skeleton of veins and smelly droppings.

The **chrysalis** is grey-green with yellow and black marks. It hibernates, and can often be found under window ledges, on walls, sheds and fences.

Habitat and behaviour

Adult Large Whites may be seen anywhere, but are commonest around vegetable gardens, allotments and cabbage fields. They will breed on any species of brassica and on garden nasturtiums, but cultivated cabbages and Brussels sprouts are its favourites.

The Large White is a highly mobile butterfly with a powerful, if somewhat fluttering flight. It does not live in identifiable colonies but flies throughout the country breeding wherever suitable conditions are encountered. In some years home-bred populations are boosted by vast swarms from the continent, and there may be return flights too, with emigrants teeming towards France.

There are generally two generations of adults a year, with the second emergence in high summer always the most numerous. After warm summers there is often a partial third brood which lasts well into October.

Distribution and status

The Large White is one of the commonest butterflies throughout the British Isles. It reaches our remotest islands, including the north Shetlands, although its survival in northern localities may be dependent on immigrants and its appearance there is consequently more erratic. It may be expected in all habitats and at all altitudes.

Numbers have always fluctuated greatly from one year to the next, but in the past it regularly occurred in devastating swarms. This is most unusual nowadays, since numbers have been depleted by a virus disease and are controlled by insecticides. Parasitic *Apanteles* wasps also kill countless caterpillars in some years.

▇▇▇ confirmed
range

73

SMALL WHITE *Pieris rapae*

Adult identification

Average wingspan 48 mm

This is the smaller of the two 'Cabbage' Whites that are common garden

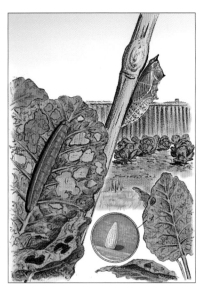

▲ *The Small White, showing its yellowish underwings and indistinctly marked wingtips. Like the Large White, its caterpillars are a familiar pest in cabbage patches throughout Europe.*

pests; other features that distinguish it from the Large White are described on page 72. The underwings of both sexes are dull pale yellow, dusted with grey, and differ greatly from the patterned underwings of our two other medium-sized White butterflies – the Green-veined White and female Orange Tip (page 30). The upperwings of the Small White are clear white (except in Ireland where they may be yellowish) with black markings that differ slightly between the sexes and in the two generations. The first brood, in spring, is much more faintly marked. The males, indeed, may be pure white, but usually the summer markings of dark wingtips, dark scales near the body, and a black spot in the middle of the forewing can be seen as faint grey marks. The female has all these marks plus an extra

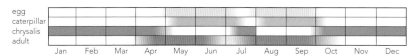

	Jan	Feb	Mar	Apr	May	Jun	Jul	Aug	Sep	Oct	Nov	Dec
egg												
caterpillar												
chrysalis												
adult												

spot on the upper forewing and a faint grey streak along its lower edge.

Young stages

The **egg** is pale yellow, bottled-shaped, and simple to find beneath the leaves of brassicas (especially cabbages) and wild crucifers in April. Although laid singly, there may be several eggs on the same plant, but not the massive clusters of the Large White.

The **caterpillar** lives solitarily, boring first into the heart of its brassica to feed, then long after the damage has been done, emerging to rest openly along the midribs of leaves. It is then easy to find, although dark green and well camouflaged against its background.

The **chrysalis** varies from being clear green to pale brown with dark speckles. It can sometimes be found on sheds, fences and under windowsills in similar positions to the Large White chrysalis.

Habitat and behaviour

Like the Large White, this attractive butterfly is a familiar sight around cabbage patches, allotments and vegetable gardens, and is widely despised as an agricultural and garden pest. However, although its caterpillars undeniably inflict severe damage on cultivated brassicas and even on garden nasturtiums, many also feed on wild crucifers along hedgerows and in wood edges.

The Small White does not live in proper colonies, but ranges widely over town and countryside, laying eggs wherever its foodplants are found. It prefers plants that are slightly sheltered, so cabbages growing near hedgerows towards the edges of fields and, especially, in gardens are chosen. Large clusters of adults may gather in these situations, otherwise the butterfly is normally seen in ones and twos flying almost anywhere. Both sexes are attracted by white flowers when feeding, and also in gardens by lavender. Numbers are invariably higher in the second generation and vary greatly from one year to the next. In some years their numbers are supplemented by large migrations from the continent, and after some warm summers there may be a small third brood of home-bred adults lasting well into autumn.

Distribution and status

This is a very common butterfly that may be found from April to October almost anywhere in England, Wales and Ireland. It is equally common in southern Scotland, but becomes much more localized on the mainland in the north. It seldom if ever reaches the outer Isles, such as Shetland and the Outer Hebrides, but is common on islands in the south such as the Isle of Man, Isle of Wight, Anglesey and the Scillies.

▨ confirmed range

GREEN-VEINED WHITE *Pieris napi*

Adult identification

Average wingspan 50 mm but smaller adults are common.

This common, medium-sized White butterfly looks very like a Small White

▲ *The spectacular underwings of the Green-veined White are clearly visible as it feeds on nectar.*

when flying, but at rest broad grey-green stripes along the veins of the underwings distinguish it from all other butterflies. This veining, which gives the butterfly its name, is highly conspicuous on all adults except for second (summer) brood females, when it is rather faint (page 30).

When the wings are open, note that the tips of the upper forewings have dark marks extending further down the outer edge than on the Small White (page 31), and that the veins are picked out as fine grey lines on all adults except first (spring) brood males. Upperwing markings are always heavier on second brood adults: the males then have a spot in the middle of each forewing whilst the females have two large spots, the lower of which merges with a black streak along the forewing's lower edge, rather like a miniature female Large White (page 31).

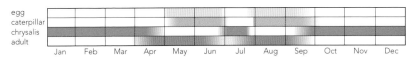

	Jan	Feb	Mar	Apr	May	Jun	Jul	Aug	Sep	Oct	Nov	Dec
egg												
caterpillar												
chrysalis												
adult												

Young stages

The **egg** is pale, bottle-shaped and laid singly. It can be found quite easily on the under-surfaces of wild crucifer leaves, often on very small plants and usually in damp places.

The **caterpillar** is dark green, with yellow rings round the spiracles but lacking the yellow stripe found on the Small White's caterpillar. Although well camouflaged, given persistent searching it can be discovered feeding on the stems and leaves of its foodplant.

The **chrysalis** is formed out of sight among dense vegetation. It comes in various colour forms ranging from green to pale brown, but all are well camouflaged and difficult to find.

Habitat and behaviour

The Green-veined White has a weak fluttering flight, but is nevertheless quite mobile. In most regions it does not live in identifiable colonies, but flies over wide areas searching for mates and breeding sites. However, unlike our two 'Cabbage' Whites, it is not a true migrant; odd individuals may be seen flying across any habitat, even dry heaths and open chalk downland, but by and large they congregate around their breeding sites. There, at best, it will be seen in hundreds, especially in the second (August) brood which is the most numerous. In the south, there are usually two broods of adults which overlap and may be seen any time from late April to September, peaking in late May and, dramatically, in early August. There is occasionally a small third brood in late September. At high altitudes and on northern islands, there may only be a single emergence in June and July.

Search for them in damp, uncultivated places, such as boggy meadows, riversides, ditches, lush hedgebanks and verges, and the rides and edges of woods. The caterpillars feed on a range of crucifers growing in humid spots, including water cress (*Nasturtium officinale*), lady's smock (*Cardamine pratensis*), garlic mustard (*Alliaria petiolata*) and hedge mustard (*Sisymbrium officinale*).

Distribution and status

The Green-veined White is frequently overlooked due to its similarity to the Small White. It is, in fact, one of our commonest and most widely distributed butterflies, although absent from the Shetlands and some areas of the central and north-west Highlands on the Scottish mainland. On a local scale, it has undoubtedly suffered greatly in recent years from drainage and agricultural improvements. Even so, small numbers survive along ditches, banks and swampy corners, even in the most intensively cultivated regions.

■ confirmed range

Adult identification

Average wingspan 45 mm (♂) to 50 mm (♀)
The male Orange Tip is unmistakable:

▲ *A freshly emerged male Orange Tip perches on one of the caterpillar's principal foodplants, lady's smock. Only the male has distinctive orange wingtips.*

a medium-sized White butterfly with bright orange wingtips. The female is less conspicuous, with grey-black tipped wings instead of orange, and a large black spot in the centre of each upper forewing. On the undersides, the hindwing is similar in both sexes, with a mottled, moss-green pattern, looking like lichen against a white background.

In flight, the female looks remarkably similar to a Small or Green-veined White, but the Orange Tip is slightly greener. At rest, her underwings are unmistakable, and no other White has a fuzzy dark central spot near the leading edge of each upper forewing. On the continent, there are several species of Orange Tip, whilst the ten species of Dappled or Bath Whites resemble the female.

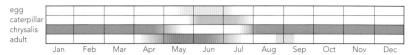

	Jan	Feb	Mar	Apr	May	Jun	Jul	Aug	Sep	Oct	Nov	Dec
egg												
caterpillar												
chrysalis												
adult												

Young stages

The **egg** is bottle-shaped and very easy to find in late May and June. It is laid singly beneath flowerbuds on the caterpillar's foodplants, and is white at first but soon turns bright orange.

The **caterpillar** is long, thin and tubular, pale orange with black hairs when young, but eventually becoming blue-green on top and dark green underneath, with inconspicuous hairs. It lies along the top of a seedpod of its foodplant and, although beautifully camouflaged, is very easy to find at all ages through June and early July.

The **caterpillar** leaves its plant to pupate among dense vegetation, and the chrysalis is almost impossible to find. It has an elegant triangular shape and is normally pale brown, although sometimes clear green.

Habitat and behaviour

The greatest concentrations of both sexes of Orange Tip are seen where there is an abundance of the caterpillar's food, which is the flowers and seedpods of tall crucifers. Much the commonest plants used are lady's smock (*Cardamine pratensis*) and garlic mustard (*Alliaria petiolata*). The former grows mainly in damp places and on heavy soils, often in tall open grassland and in woodland rides; the latter prefers drier conditions along hedgerows, banks, wood edges, and wasteland, especially on calcareous soils. Between them, these crucifers support Orange Tips over a wide range of habitats, although boggy meadows with abundant lady's smock are scarce nowadays, and the grubbing up of hedgerows has greatly reduced garlic mustard in some flat regions. Additional foodplants are hedge mustard and, less often, charlock, watercress and honesty.

Adult Orange Tips are quite mobile. They are not confined to self-contained colonies, and the males may be seen almost anywhere within their range, flitting slowly between white objects in their quest for females. The latter are more secretive (and often dismissed as Small Whites), but their roamings are betrayed by the presence of eggs even on the remotest and most isolated of foodplants.

Distribution and status

Despite some local declines, the Orange Tip is a common butterfly throughout Ireland, Wales, and England, except for the north-east, where it is mainly confined to damp valleys. In Scotland it remains somewhat localized despite expanding greatly in range during recent warm decades, and is absent from the Highlands (apart from sheltered glens) and the far north, and from all of the Scottish Isles.

On the continent it is also a common butterfly throughout most countries.

▒▒▒ confirmed range

GREEN HAIRSTREAK *Callophrys rubi*

Adult identification

Average wingspan 33 mm (15 mm closed)

An unmistakable little butterfly that always sits with its wings closed, display-

▲ *The Green Hairstreak is conspicuous when perching on bluebells or other spring flowers, but is beautifully camouflaged when it settles on leaves.*

ing their bright green undersides. Small areas of the plain brown uppersides are sometimes visible where the wings overlap. The tail is reduced to a stump in this Hairstreak, and the two sexes look much the same. In flight, the impression is of brown blurred wings, rather like a Dingy Skipper or female Blue, but at rest it is unmistakable.

In south-east France, Chapman's Green Hairstreak is slightly larger, with a white line across the green undersides, but is otherwise almost identical.

Young stages

It is almost impossible to find wild **eggs**, which are glassy, pale green, flattened spheres and inserted singly into the tender leaf tips or flower buds of the butterfly's foodplants.

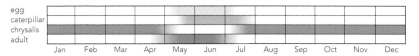

	Jan	Feb	Mar	Apr	May	Jun	Jul	Aug	Sep	Oct	Nov	Dec
egg												
caterpillar												
chrysalis												
adult												

The **caterpillar**, when fully grown, is shaped like a large fleshy woodlouse, with distinct segments. It is green with yellow markings, and is hard to spot even though it lives openly among the young leaf or flower tips of its various foodplants.

Secretions make the ground-living **chrysalis** attractive to ants, but it is very hard to find except, by chance, under flat stones containing ant nests. It is deep brown and quite hairy.

Habitat and behaviour

The Green Hairstreak is found in many habitats, including moorland, lowland heath, chalk and limestone downs, woods, embankments, and rough scrubby wasteland. Typical colonies contain fewer than 50 adults. The eggs are laid on a wide range of plants, from low-growing herbs to shrubs. The main foods are bilberry (*Vaccinium myrtillus*) on moors, gorses (all *Ulex* spp.) on acid and neutral soils, and rockrose (*Helianthemum chamaecistus*) on calcareous grassland. Dyer's green-weed, bird's-foot trefoil, and dogwood and buckthorn flowers are often used elsewhere. The common feature of most sites is that they contain scattered shrubs and are warm and sheltered; many are hillsides.

The males are territorial and perch in the sunshine on prominent shrubs, usually one per bush, in the lowest parts of sites, where they await the females. It is always easy to find the males by examining suitable bushes. When disturbed, they are hard to follow for they make rapid jerky flights among the shrubs, but invariably return to the same perches and can then be closely approached. The females are much less obvious, and fly inconspicuously over larger areas to lay their eggs.

Distribution and status

This is our most widely distributed Hairstreak. Colonies may be expected in suitable habitat throughout Ireland, west Wales, south-west England and west Scotland, where it remains a local, yet common butterfly; huge populations occasionally develop in warm gorse-filled valleys and on some bilberry moors. Elsewhere in Britain the Green Hairstreak has become much more localized, although it is still frequently encountered in most southern English counties, especially on heaths. In central and eastern England, it is reduced to a handful of colonies per county, mostly around woods or on embankments.

The Green Hairstreak was very much commoner until quite recently, but countless colonies have been lost through the reclamation or improvement of old grassland, heaths and moors, through intensive forestry, and the general tidying up of the countryside. Throughout Europe, it remains a common butterfly of seminatural habitats.

▨ confirmed range

BROWN HAIRSTREAK *Thecla betulae*

Adult identification

Average wingspan 38 mm (♂) to 40 mm (♀)

Adults are usually seen with the wings closed, exposing bright golden under-wings crossed by two thin white lines, and a distinct tail. The female is a richer gold and has the longer tail (page 21). Brown Hairstreaks open their wings in weak sunshine: the upperwings are deep

▲ *The Brown Hairstreak is an elusive butterfly, but the female is sometimes seen when she rests on leaves between bouts of egg-laying.*

brown, marked on the forewings with faint yellow patches in the male or large orange blotches in the female.

No other butterfly is similar seen close up or at rest, but the male Gatekeeper (page 156), flying high among the tree-tops, can be mistaken for this species. The Gatekeeper is less golden and has a slower, less erratic flight. A more usual mistake is to misidentify the male Vapourer moth, which is bright gold but smaller, and flies by day in a similar manner among treetops in late summer. It is much commoner than the Brown Hairstreak. Confirm by searching for Brown Hairstreak eggs in winter.

Young stages

The presence of this butterfly is most easily established by searching for the pin-head-sized **egg**, which is laid singly or in pairs, and looks like a tiny white bun. This is very conspicuous against the dark bark of young prominent blackthorn twigs; examine the bases of spines, or forks and notches during winter.

	Jan	Feb	Mar	Apr	May	Jun	Jul	Aug	Sep	Oct	Nov	Dec
egg												
caterpillar												
chrysalis												
adult												

The **caterpillar** has a slug-like shape in profile, but is triangular when seen head on. It is pale green with yellow stripes, and is perfectly camouflaged as it rests, upside down, beneath a blackthorn leaf. It can be found quite easily by patient searching in late June.

The dark brown, featureless **chrysalis** is almost impossible to find. It is formed on the ground among leaf litter or in crevices, and is sometimes tended by ants.

Habitat and behaviour

Colonies are found mainly in well-wooded districts, especially on heavy soils, or in slightly hilly areas where there are numerous small hedged fields containing a high proportion of blackthorn among the shrubs. Typical colonies are quite small and are centred on a wood, where the adults congregate for mating year after year on the crown of a tall prominent 'master' tree, often an ash. The males rarely descend, or indeed fly, obtaining their food from aphid honeydew on the treetops. After mating, the females soon disperse to lay their eggs, singly, low down on blackthorn (*Prunus spinosa*) or any other *Prunus* they encounter. They fly over a very wide area around the master tree, laying at low densities on young prominent growths along wood edges and, particularly, hedges. Nearly all the adults seen will be egg-laying females, but even these are secretive, flying seldom and hugging the hedgerows. The egg, on the other hand, is very easy to find in the first months of winter after the leaves have fallen. By spring most will have been destroyed by hedge trimming.

Distribution and status

The Brown Hairstreak is a scarce butterfly that has disappeared from many regions, but is often overlooked. In Ireland, it is well distributed around the Burren but probably, nowadays, nowhere else. It is also extinct in Scotland and northern England. There are, however, three areas of abundance in southern England, and another in Wales, where eggs may be expected on any suitable-looking hedge. Look for it in Wales in the little wooded valleys throughout the south-west, and in Devon in a band of similar habitat extending from the vales between Exmoor and Dartmoor as far as the Polden Hills in Somerset. The third concentration is in the West Weald of Surrey and Sussex, among the extensive woods on the clays. Elsewhere, it is abundant east of Oxford, and occasional colonies survive in southern English counties, mainly on heavy soils, but very few survive north of Oxford except in a pocket of north Lincolnshire. Numerous extinctions have occurred in the flatter parts of southern England, notably in East Anglia. These, no doubt, are victims of the loss of hedgerows and other scrubby areas.

▧▧▧ confirmed
range

PURPLE HAIRSTREAK *Neozephyrus quercus*

Adult identification

Average wingspan 37 mm (♀) to 39 mm (♂)

A beautiful butterfly, with inky black upperwings that turn deep purple as they catch the sun. In the male, this colour is deeper and occurs over all the

▲ *The adult Purple Hairstreak spends most of its life perched, with wings closed, on the top of an oak tree.*

wings apart from the margins; the purple on females is a large blotch on each forewing, which is visible even in dull light. The underwings are silver-grey with a white streak and a single black-pupilled orange eye beside the tail.

No other butterfly is similar when seen close to. In flight, a White-letter Hairstreak (page 86), Holly Blue (page 106) or Common Blue (page 100) high above the treetops will also reflect the sun, but there is no mistaking the Purple Hairstreak's alternate glint of silver and purple, spinning in the sky above the canopy. On the continent, only the Spanish Purple Hairstreak in the Iberian Peninsula is similar.

Young stages

The **egg** usually occurs singly and is very easy to find at the base of fat flower buds or on twigs on sunny parts of mature oaks. Look for small grey pin-head-sized

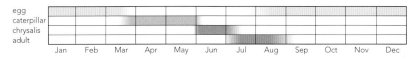

	Jan	Feb	Mar	Apr	May	Jun	Jul	Aug	Sep	Oct	Nov	Dec
egg												
caterpillar												
chrysalis												
adult												

discs during winter after the leaves have been shed (page 13).

On hatching in spring, the **caterpillar** enters bursting oak buds on which it feeds. Later, it lives inside a silk web spun round the base of a leaf clump, which traps the leaf scales. It emerges at night to browse on leaves. Although perfectly camouflaged by day, the brown, seg-mented, woodlouse-shaped caterpillar is easy to find in June by feeling the bases of leaf clumps until one feels spongy.

The **chrysalis** can sometimes be found deep inside ant nests among tussocks of grass or under moss at the base of oaks. It is reddish-brown with dark freckles, and produces secretions that attract ants.

Habitat and behaviour

The Purple Hairstreak lives in discrete colonies that fluctuate enormously in size from year to year. A single mature oak tree of any *Quercus* species can support a colony, but most populations are cen-tred on woods. Although often abundant, the adults are hard to see from the ground, for most of their lives are spent perched on the canopy; tapping the lower boughs often dislodges a few, and occasionally hundreds, of Purple Hairstreaks. However, this butterfly is usually seen in ones or twos, as silver specks tumbling in the sky above the treetops. Egg-laying occurs on bushy growth all over the canopy and down to ground level, with particularly high densities laid on sunny sheltered boughs.

Distribution and status

The Purple Hairstreak is much commoner than is generally realized. It probably occurs in every wood with a reasonable number of oaks throughout Wales and in England south of the Wash. In warm years, the larger oakwoods of these regions support tens or even hundreds of thousands of adults. Smaller numbers will be found in many copses and spinneys, in plantations with occasional oaks, and, less often, on isolated parkland, garden or hedgerow trees. Further north, the Purple Hairstreak is much more localized, although often overlooked, especially in Scotland. Whilst it has spread recently on its northern boundaries, numerous colonies have been destroyed where oakwoods have been replaced by conifer planta-tions, yet small numbers usually persist if nurse trees or cosmetic oaks have been spared. Similarly, it is worth searching any deciduous wood in the south that contains more than one or two oaks.

Colonies of Purple Hairstreak are scarce in Ireland, occurring mainly in hillside oakwoods between Wicklow and Derry, and are common in woods throughout Europe, although naturally absent from the conifer forests of north Scandinavia.

▦ confirmed range

85

WHITE-LETTER HAIRSTREAK *Satyrium w-album*

Adult identification

Average wingspan 36 mm (16 mm closed)

This is our darkest Hairstreak. Both sexes look similar, although females tend to have longer tails. The wings are never opened, except to fly, so only the

▲ *This recently emerged White-letter Hairstreak, with its long wing-tails still intact, has made a rare descent from the treetops to feed on flowers.*

underwings are usually visible. These are blackish-brown, with a thin white line across each wing often, but not always, shaped like a W on its side opposite the tail. There is also a band of orange crescents near the edge of the hindwing.

The rare Black Hairstreak is very similar – see pages 33 and 88 for distinguishing features. In flight, high above a treetop, the White-letter Hairstreak's wings catch the sun and can easily be mistaken for the silver glint of a Purple Hairstreak (page 84). On the continent, it may also be confused with the Sloe, Ilex, False Ilex, and Blue Spot Hairstreaks.

Young stages

One of the easiest ways to find a colony is to search for **eggs** during winter. Look for a single grey disc, shaped like a minute flying saucer, fixed below a flower bud or on a twig on the sunny side of the canopy of a mature elm.

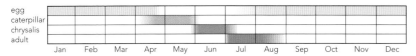

	Jan	Feb	Mar	Apr	May	Jun	Jul	Aug	Sep	Oct	Nov	Dec
egg												
caterpillar												
chrysalis												
adult												

At first the **caterpillar** enters an elm flower, on which it feeds, but soon moves to the base of a leaf cluster and thereafter eats leaves. The fully grown caterpillar is clear green and lies exposed on the surface of a leaf. It is beautifully camouflaged, but can be spotted quite easily from below in early June by its dark slug-like silhouette.

The **chrysalis** is dark and very hairy, like the elm twig against which it is often fixed. With practice, it can be found in June.

Habitat and behaviour

Few butterflies are more elusive than this attractive Hairstreak; it is easier to find the young stages than the adult. The caterpillars feed on the flowers and leaves of elm (*Ulmus* spp.), and may be found on any species, especially wych elm. Breeding occurs on trees, not clipped elm hedges, although a single isolated hedgerow tree will often support a colony; it is worth examining even a young sucker, especially if large enough to flower. However, the butterfly will more often be found on a tall bushy tree or on a clump of elms growing in a sunny sheltered position, especially along a wood edge.

Colonies tend to be very small, punctuated by occasional years of abundance. Both males and females spend most of their lives perched high on a treetop, where they bask and drink aphid honeydew. Periodically, an individual will loop high above the canopy in a rapid jerky flight, soon to return to its original bough. Less often one may descend to feed on a flower, where it can be closely approached. In warm still weather, watch also for females flying at all levels over the canopy to lay their eggs.

Distribution and status

Despite the widespread loss of elms through Dutch elm disease, the White-letter Hairstreak remains widely distributed through most of Wales and England, extending well into Yorkshire. Although local everywhere, colonies are often overlooked, and probably now occur in their greatest abundance in the east English Midlands, having declined greatly in its former stronghold of the West Midlands and Welsh borders. The White-letter Hairstreak seems to be surviving best on wych elms, especially towards the extremes of its range, for example in Nottinghamshire and further north, and in the West Country. Many colonies establish on rejuvenating elm growth, even immature suckers, but tend to die out as the infected elms grow tall and die.

On the continent the White-letter Hairstreak has experienced similar losses, having recently been locally common across the whole of central Europe.

confirmed range

BLACK HAIRSTREAK *Satyrium pruni*

Adult identification

Average wingspan 37 mm (16 mm closed)

Both sexes of this rarity look much the same and, since the wings are never opened except in flight, only the underwings are visible. These are brown with a golden sheen and a conspicuous thin white line down each wing, halfway in. The diagnostic feature is an orange border

▲ *The rare Black Hairstreak often perches on the caterpillar's foodplant, blackthorn. Despite the name, it is paler and more golden than the White-letter Hairstreak.*

towards the edge of the wings which contains a row of black spots. The tail is quite pronounced. The White-letter Hairstreak (page 86) is often mistaken for this butterfly; note that the white line opposite the tail can be shaped like a sideways 'W' in both species. The White-letter Hairstreak is the darker butterfly but does not have a row of black spots near the wing edges. Silhouetted on a treetop, the White-letter Hairstreak looks slightly more triangular, and note, too, the limited geographical range of the Black Hairstreak.

Young stages

The **egg** is an orange-brown flattened disc, covered with minute radiating spikes, and is laid singly at all heights on blackthorn twigs. It can be found, none too easily, during winter.

The **caterpillar** changes much in its appearance as it grows, from deep chestnut, to chestnut with a white saddle, then becoming greener, and finally translucent green with pale stripes and pink tips to

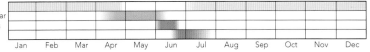

	Jan	Feb	Mar	Apr	May	Jun	Jul	Aug	Sep	Oct	Nov	Dec
egg												
caterpillar												
chrysalis												
adult												

the ridges down its back. It may be found perfectly camouflaged on its food: first on unopened buds, then lying across the bursting scales, and finally exposed in full sunshine among a bunch of fresh leaves.

Marginally the easiest stage to find, the **chrysalis** resembles a bird dropping and is found exposed on top of a blackthorn leaf or, more usually, on a half-shaded twig.

Habitat and behaviour

Typical colonies contain a few adults and are strictly confined to very small areas of a wood or adjoining hedgerow. Any species of *Prunus* can be used for breeding, but blackthorn (*P. spinosa*) is usual. Tall, sunny, sheltered banks of mature, lichen-encrusted plants are its commonest habitat, although some very large colonies have been supported entirely by young growth. Look for this butterfly, within its range, wherever sunny stands of *Prunus* occur along sheltered wood edges, glades or rides, in tall adjoining hedgerows, or as scrub near woods.

The adults seldom fly and almost never stray, preferring to live most of their lives perched out of sight on treetops or tall blackthorns, where they drink aphid honeydew. It is easy to miss a colony; use binoculars and look, too, for its jerky flight as it seems to hop around the top of a tall bank of blackthorn. Eventually, an adult will descend to perch or feed on privet blossom or other flowers, and then it can be approached very closely.

Distribution and status

The Black Hairstreak is a rare butterfly and is confined to the woods of the East Midlands forest belt, in the basin of heavy clays that lies between Peterborough and Oxford. About 30 colonies remain out of about 60 ever recorded; a good rate of survival compared with most butterflies.

Because of their small breeding areas and sedentary behaviour, colonies are usually lost during large-scale modern forestry operations; in the past they were similarly vulnerable to the short coppice cycles that were prevalent in much of Britain outside the East Midlands. Today, survival in its traditional woods depends largely on conservation measures, and several fine colonies breed on County Trust and Forest Enterprise Reserves. Elsewhere in Britain, there are probably many places on heavy soils where the Black Hairstreak could breed nowadays, if it could reach them; for example, one introduced colony in the Weald of Surrey recently flourished near Cranleigh for about 35 years, but is now believed to be extinct

In Europe, the Black Hairstreak is found very locally in central regions from northern Spain, across central France, Switzerland and Austria, and more widely in Greece and the Balkans. A few colonies occur in Denmark, Sweden and Finland.

▓▓▓ confirmed
range

Adult identification

Average wingspan 32 mm (♂) to 35 mm (♀)

feeding groove

▲ *The typical basking posture of a Small Copper with its wings held wide open.*

Both sexes of the little Small Copper butterfly are similar and easy to identify. The upperwings are brilliant: shining copper with black marks and borders on the forewings, and copper borders against a black background on the hindwings. The underwings are equally distinctive: the hindwing is grey-brown whilst the forewing is pale orange with black spots.

Everywhere there is a good deal of variation in the size of the black marks on the upperwings. In central and northern Scotland and in Ireland there is always less black and more clear copper, and Irish underwings tend to be grey. Throughout its range, there is a variety that has a row of blue spots on the upper hindwings; these beautiful specimens are rare in most areas but

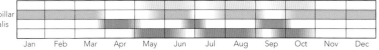

	Jan	Feb	Mar	Apr	May	Jun	Jul	Aug	Sep	Oct	Nov	Dec
egg												
caterpillar												
chrysalis												
adult												

comprise up to half the adults in parts of northern Scotland.

Nothing in Britain can be confused with this butterfly either in flight or at rest. On the continent there are several other small copper-coloured butterflies.

Young stages

Looking like a tiny, white golf ball, the **egg** is very easy to find on small young sorrel leaves. Look along the midrib, especially near the stem on the upper-surface.

On hatching, the **caterpillar** eats small conspicuous grooves on the underside of a sorrel leaf. When older, it is slug-like and plain green, often with a pink edge. It rests beneath a leaf, and is quite easy to find at all ages.

The **chrysalis** is very hard to spot in the wild. It is pale brown, flecked with dark specks, and is formed among dead leaf litter.

Habitat and behaviour

This is a conspicuous little butterfly, common in rough open places. It lives in more or less discrete colonies which are usually small: larger numbers emerge in the second (August) brood, but even then it is generally seen in ones and twos. After warm summers, a third or even a small fourth brood may emerge in the south, with adults flying late into October. Colonies may be found in open situations on all soils where the foodplants grow. Look especially on ancient grazed grassland, heaths, wasteland, dunes and cliffs, in old pits and quarries, and along sunny woodland rides, embankments and road verges; it is not unusual to find it nectaring in gardens.

The eggs are laid on common sorrel (*Rumex acetosa*) or sheep's sorrel (*R. acetosella*) and very occasionally on docks. First-brood eggs are often laid on quite large, though tender, sorrel leaves, growing in grass up to 0.3 m tall. In the second brood small plants are greatly preferred, such as develop on unstable or disturbed land, in well-grazed fields, or after a hay crop.

Distribution and status

The Small Copper has declined greatly in many areas, notably in flat regions, due to the intensification of agriculture, the increased shadiness of most woods, the reclamation of heathland, and the lack of sheep or rabbit grazing on unimproved downs. Nevertheless, it is still a common butterfly and may be expected throughout the British Isles wherever its habitats occur. It is absent only from high mountains, parts of northern Scotland, and the outer Scottish Isles.

In Europe, it is also one of the commonest butterflies.

▬ confirmed range

SMALL OR LITTLE BLUE *Cupido minimus*

Adult identification

Wingspan variable: 20 mm–30 mm, average 24 mm

This, our smallest butterfly, is easy to identify. The tiny upperwings have no pattern – females are dark brown, males smokey-black with a dusting of silvery-blue

▲ *The Small Blue usually basks with its wings half open after egg-laying, allowing the sooty upperwings, clear white fringes, and silver underwings to be seen.*

scales near the body. The fringes are clear white with no veining. The underwings are very distinctive – silver-grey with a scattering of tiny black dots (like a miniature Holly Blue, page 106) and none of the orange markings found on other Blues.

Although unmistakable at rest, its silvery wings resemble the two Brown Arguses (pages 96–99) during flight. On the continent, Osiris Blue and Lorquin's Blue are very similar, except that the males' upperwings are clear blue.

Young stages

The **egg** is more easily found than any stage, including the adult. Gently part the 'fingers' of kidney vetch flowers in June and look for tiny pale blue discs. There will often be two or three per flowerhead, laid singly by different females.

The young **caterpillar** disappears into a flower (by then a seedcase) to feed on young tissue, but by late July lives openly

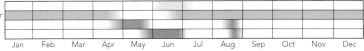

	Jan	Feb	Mar	Apr	May	Jun	Jul	Aug	Sep	Oct	Nov	Dec
egg												
caterpillar												
chrysalis												
adult												

on the seedhead: look for a pale pinkish-grey grub with its head buried deep into a seed capsule. The fully grown caterpillar deserts its plant in high summer to hibernate in a crevice on the ground. Nine months later the **chrysalis** is formed – grey, black spotted and rather hairy – and, like the hibernating caterpillar, almost impossible to find.

Habitat and behaviour

The Small Blue lives in small close-knit colonies in warm sheltered hollows and nooks where the grass is tall enough for kidney vetch (*Anthyllis vulneraria*) to flower, yet not so dense that the food-plant ever becomes swamped. Typical sites are the sparse south-facing sides of abandoned chalk and lime pits, embankments, broken cliffs and coombes on downs. Open grassland is very rarely occupied, except in the Cotswolds. Thus the butterfly has a very much more restricted distribution than its foodplant, and even this is not particularly common, being confined to well-drained, base-rich soils, particularly chalk and lime.

Most colonies consist of a few tens of adults which fly and breed in the same few square metres of ground year after year. It is thus easy to miss a colony, especially since these small dark butterflies are more secretive than Britain's other Blues. The males, especially, prefer to perch for long periods on tussocks or shrubs. They bask with the wings half open, and fly briefly only to intercept a passing female. There is often a small second brood of adults on southern sites, generally in August.

Distribution and status

The Small Blue is widely distributed in Britain, but extremely rare through most of its range. In Scotland, there are one or two inland colonies and perhaps a dozen more

along the north and north-east coast, but it is probably extinct in the south-east Borders. It is even rarer in north England and has not been seen in the Peak District since the 1990s. In Wales it is virtually confined to the southern coastline where, however, it is locally common. It is probably extinct in Northern Ireland, but persists in occasional small colonies along the west and south-east coasts. Nearly all surviving English colonies are on the southern chalk and limestone hills, with the Cotswolds, with 145 known colonies, being its stronghold; there alone the Small Blue may be expected on most unfertilized hills where there is kidney vetch, including open downland. The next best areas are Salisbury Plain (Wiltshire) and the chalk and limestone hills of Dorset and the Isle of Wight. In other southern counties it is very much more localized, although present in most up to and including the Chilterns. Its absence from the Devon and Cornish coastline, despite the abundance of kidney vetch, is a curiosity.

▓▓▓ confirmed
range

93

SILVER-STUDDED BLUE *Plebejus argus*

Adult identification

Average wingspan 29 mm (♂) to 31 mm (♀)

This comparatively small Blue lives mainly on heaths. Distinguishing features of the male's upperwings are the deep blue ground colour and clear white fringes, contrasting with a black border that is much wider than on male Com-

▲ *A pair of Silver-studded Blues perch on heather to mate. The male has broad black borders to his blue upperwings, whilst the female's underwings are equally distinctive (page 15).*

mon, Holly or Adonis Blues (pages 34–35). His silver underwings are more distinctive; note, on the hindwing the broad band of orange near the edge adjoining black eyespots, each with a tiny bright blue-green pupil. These 'studs' are found on no other Blue and give the butterfly its name. On the under forewing, there is no spot nearer to the body than halfway in, unlike the spotting on Common, Adonis and Chalkhill Blues.

The female upperwings are dark brown. Although often tinged with blue near the body (especially in northern colonies), she is frequently muddled with the two Brown Arguses (pages 96–99). Examine the underwings, which have the same blue-studded eyes and broad orange band as the male, but on a deep brown background. Her other black spots are unusually large for a Blue, and the pair near the top corner of the hindwing are horizontal (..) rather than the colon (:) of Brown Arguses.

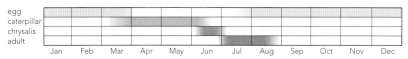

	Jan	Feb	Mar	Apr	May	Jun	Jul	Aug	Sep	Oct	Nov	Dec
egg												
caterpillar												
chrysalis												
adult												

Young stages

The **egg**, a white disc with minute spikes (page 7), is laid singly in midsummer but hibernates until spring. Search for it low down in sparse patches of young gorse and heather shoots sprouting from bare sand. On limestone it can be found in cracks where bird's-foot trefoil and other foodplants grow between stones covering black ant (*Lasius niger*) nests.

The **caterpillar** is well camouflaged, but sometimes seen browsing young leaf-tips in the evening, always attended by black ants. When fully grown, it is green with a dark line down the back, olive and white stripes on the flanks, and shaped like a fleshy woodlouse. Although easily found in black ant nests, take great care not to damage the fragile habitat of this rare butterfly.

The **chrysalis** is pale brown and buried underground by ants. It can also be found inside ant nests, but up to half hatch into beautiful parasitic wasps rather than butterflies.

Habitat and behaviour

This is a sedentary butterfly that lives in discrete colonies. Nearly all are on heathland, breeding – especially in the north – on regenerating growth in recent clearings and burnt areas, or in degenerate patches where the heather is leggy and light reaches the ground. In its southern strongholds, most heathland colonies are confined to damp hollows and along rills, where the heather grows sparsely – it is generally absent from mature heaths. The caterpillars eat a range of plants, including heathers (*Calluna vulgaris*, *Erica* spp.), gorse (all *Ulex* spp.) and bird's-foot trefoil (*Lotus corniculatus*), but feed only on tender leafsprouts with black ants nearby. Dunes can also support fine populations. Although no colony survives on chalk downland, several exist on limestone cliffs, where the vegetation grows sparsely among rocks and rubble, and where the caterpillars eat bird's-foot trefoil, rockroses (*Helianthemum* spp.) and other low-growing shoots. As on young heathland, some limestone colonies are vast, containing tens of thousands of adults.

Distribution and status

This beautiful Blue has become a great rarity in most regions of Britain – countless colonies have been destroyed or shaded out in recent decades. Today, a few populations survive on the heaths of Norfolk, Suffolk, and north Wales, and on dunes along the coasts of Devon, Cornwall and south Wales. The great majority, however, are on the acid heaths of Sussex, Surrey, Hampshire and Dorset. In the New Forest and Dorset it is still locally common, sometimes abundant, wherever open 'humid' heathland survives. Large populations also occur on limestone on Anglesey and in north-west Wales, and in old quarries and undercliffs on Portland, Dorset.

confirmed
range

BROWN ARGUS *Aricia agestis*

Adult identification

Average wingspan 29 mm

Both sexes look similar. The upperwings are sooty brown, slightly darker in males, with a black spot in the centre of each forewing and no trace of blue, unlike the female Common Blue. Round the edges is

▲ *A female Brown Argus basking on a southern English chalk down. In recent years it has also spread to agri-environmental farmland.*

a series of orange crescents that are generally larger on the female. The fringes are white, sometimes just penetrated with brown veins. The underwings resemble those of Silver-studded, Common, Adonis, and Chalkhill Blues, but differ from the last three in lacking any spot on the forewing nearer than halfway in to the body, and from all by the spots at the top edge of the hindwing, which form a colon (:); see pages 34–35. In flight, adults appear surprisingly silvery. The Northern Brown Argus (page 98) is generally identical, but hardly over-laps in range and seldom in emergence date, and in many races lacks black pupils to the white eyes on the underwings whilst the central spot on the upper forewings is white rather than black. Nearly all Brown Argus colonies have two generations a year, each of similar abundance, but there is a confusing region in the Peak District and Yorkshire Wolds, near the southern boundary of the Northern Brown Argus, where both butterflies are single brooded.

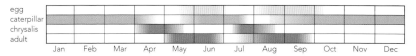

	Jan	Feb	Mar	Apr	May	Jun	Jul	Aug	Sep	Oct	Nov	Dec
egg												
caterpillar												
chrysalis												
adult												

Young stages

The **egg** is a pale white disc, laid singly on the undersides of the largest, most tender leaves and on the stems of rockroses, storksbill or geranium. It is quite easy to find in late May and again in August in strong colonies.

The **caterpillar** feeds first on the under-surfaces of the egg plant leaves, making minute perforations from beneath, leaving the upper cuticle intact. These windows are easy to spot, but be warned, some beetles cause similar damage. Older caterpillars feed openly by day on whole leaves, but are beautifully camouflaged being fleshy green with a pink stripe round the edge. They can be found, not very easily, in April and July by searching for the excited ants that invariably attend them.

The **chrysalis** is pale brown and buried by ants in an earth cell, making it very hard to find.

Habitat and behaviour

The Brown Argus lives in small colonies, mostly on chalk and limestone grassland, where the caterpillar's main food, common rockrose (*Helianthemum chamaecistus*), is abundant. Typical sites are steep south-facing downs, banks or earthworks, where the soil is thin and the vegetation sparse or cropped quite short. Colonies also occur on calcareous dunes and cliffs, and in woods, heaths and on recently aban-doned heavier soils. On these latter sites, common storksbill (*Erodium cicutarium*) and dove's-foot cranesbill (*Geranium molle*) are eaten instead. Once a rarity, these 'storksbill colonies' have spread greatly since the 1980s, especially in East Anglia and Lincolnshire where agri-environmental farmland schemes generated a vast mosaic of suitable sites.

Whatever the habitat, the females fly freely over open ground while the males perch in sheltered hollows and at the base of hills. Like most Blues, they roost com-munally and can be found at dusk or dawn on sheltered clumps of grass.

Distribution and status

The Brown Argus is a local butterfly that is largely confined to the south-eastern half of England and to the Welsh coast. In England, 'storksbill colonies' are now widespread throughout its range, and have spread locally across East Anglia, Lincolnshire and into Yorkshire. It remains absent, however, from most of west England and Wales, apart from the calcareous dunes and grasslands of the Devon, Cornwall, and north and south Wales coasts. Most colonies are still found locally on chalk and limestone downs in the Cotswolds, the Chilterns, the edges of Salisbury Plain, the North Downs escarpment in Kent and Surrey, the South Downs of Sussex, and on the chalk of Dorset and the Isle of Wight.

▓▓ confirmed range

Adult identification

Average wingspan 29 mm

Both sexes of this dusky little butterfly look much the same and almost identical to the Brown Argus. Geography and flight period separate these two species, but they may usually also be distinguished by the presence of a con-

▲ *In Scotland, where this photograph was taken, the Northern Brown Argus has gleaming white marks on the forewings and indistinct spots on the underwings.*

spicuous white spot in the centre of each upper forewing on the Northern Brown Argus. Note, however that this feature is absent or reduced in most English colonies. The underwings are also less heavily marked than on the Brown Argus, although the pattern is the same; for example, there is often no black dot in the centre of the white spots, especially in Scotland.

This butterfly may be distinguished from other Blues by the features described for the Brown Argus (page 96). Note also that its range overlaps only with Small and Common Blues among the 'brown' Blues. The Small Blue has no orange on either sides of the wings and quite different silver undersides; the Common Blue has mainly 'blue' females in these northerly localities.

Young stages

The **egg** is a white disc, similar to that of the Brown Argus but laid on the top

	Jan	Feb	Mar	Apr	May	Jun	Jul	Aug	Sep	Oct	Nov	Dec
egg												
caterpillar												
chrysalis												
adult												

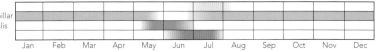

rather than beneath rockrose leaves; consequently it is much easier to find. Look for it from late June in the south, late July in east and north Scotland.

The young **caterpillar** feeds beneath the leaves making small holes with the transparent upper cuticle left intact. When fully grown it feeds exposed on rockrose and is pale green, with short white hairs and a pink stripe that is paler than on the Brown Argus running round the edge. It can be found, but none too easily, tended by ants in late May.

The **chrysalis** is well hidden, being attractive to ants and almost certainly buried in earth cells. It is a pale brownish-green colour, darker on the wing cases and thorax, with pale pink streaks on the abdomen.

Habitat and behaviour

This dark little butterfly was probably among the first to recolonize Britain after the last Ice Age. It is now restricted to the chillier parts of the north, although absent from the very coldest areas such as mountains above 350 m. It lives in small discrete colonies consisting, usually, of a few hundred individuals at most. These are found on northern limestones and other base rich soils where the caterpillar's food, common rockrose (*Helianthemum chamaecistus*), grows in abundance on south-facing exposures. Typical sites are mountains where there is broken ground or scree, eroding cliffs, or rough open grassland. Rockrose is absent on a few sites and it is believed that the caterpillars eat wild geranium on these – this is certainly an alternative food in captivity.

As with most Blues, the adults roost communally in sheltered pockets at the base of hills, perched head down on grass clumps. In weak sunshine they bask with their wings wide open allowing their dark surfaces to absorb warmth. In brighter sunlight they close their wings and the silvery undersides reflect excessive heat. When warm, they fly frequently and low down over open ground, visiting flowers and searching for rockroses.

Distribution and status

This is a very local butterfly of Scotland and northern England. Its most southerly sites are in the Lake District and north Lancashire, where numerous colonies exist on limestone outcrops. The few colonies on the Durham coast have fared less well in recent years, as have those in southern Scotland, where it persists in scattered sites in the border counties and along the south-west coast of Dumfries, Kirkcudbright, Wigtown and Ayr. It is much more widespread, and probably still overlooked, farther north in Scotland, especially in north Perthshire, Angus and Aberdeenshire, with a few colonies as far north as south-east Sutherland.

▮▮▮ confirmed
range

COMMON BLUE *Polyommatus icarus*

Adult identification

Average wingspan 35 mm (larger in the north)

This is our commonest Blue. Males have unmarked, bright blue upperwings; females orange crescents and dark spots near the outer edges on a ground colour that varies from almost entirely purple-blue to dark brown with a mere tinge of blue near the body. Irish and Scottish females

▲ *The male Common Blue basks with his wings open whenever the sunlight is weak. It lives in discrete colonies but single specimens may wander almost anywhere.*

are especially large and blue, and sometimes misidentified as Large Blues (page 108). The underwings of both sexes have numerous black spots with white haloes, and orange marks around the edges.

The following features, illustrated on pages 34–35, distinguish the Common Blue from similar Blues:

Males

- Holly Blues have silver underwings with tiny black dots.
- Silver-studded Blues have broad borders to the upperwings, and blue studs on the underwing.
- Adonis Blues are more turquoise (though in some lights look similar), with black veins across the white fringes.

Females

- Brown Argus and Northern Brown Argus have no and Silver-studded Blues little blue on the upperwings and no spot nearer to the body than halfway in on the under forewing. The under hindwings of the first two species have a colon (:) two-thirds out from the body near the top edge. The Silver-

	Jan	Feb	Mar	Apr	May	Jun	Jul	Aug	Sep	Oct	Nov	Dec
egg												
caterpillar												
chrysalis												
adult												

studded Blue has blue studs.
- Adonis and Chalkhill Blues have conspicuous dark veins across the white fringes.

Young stages

The **egg** is a small white disc, laid singly and easily found on the young terminal leaflets of bird's-foot trefoil and other foodplants (see Habitat). Search in early July and again in September in the south, and in August in the north.

The plain green **caterpillar** is slightly furry and feeds on its foodplant's leaves by day. It sits exposed on the plant, and although well camouflaged, can be found quite easily when its presence is betrayed by ants, which often attend it for its sugary secretions (page 9). Hibernation occurs when quite small, among dead leaves.

The pale green **chrysalis** is formed on the ground and soon buried by ants; it may occasionally be found inside ant nests under stones.

Habitat and behaviour

The caterpillar's usual foodplant is bird's-foot trefoil (*Lotus corniculatus*), and colonies can be expected anywhere where this grows in reasonable abundance, even in small pockets of land. Typical sites are dunes, cliffs, undercliffs, heaths, wasteland, old quarries, downs and any rough unfertilized grassland that is cropped fairly short. Small colonies are common in overgrown boggy fields and along ditches where marsh bird's-foot trefoil (*L. uliginosus*) is eaten; breeding also occurs on restharrows (*Ononis* spp.) and especially black medick (*Medicago lupulina*).

The butterfly lives in discrete colonies, although adults occasionally wander and may be encountered anywhere, including gardens. In the south there are usually two adult broods, and occasionally a third in early autumn. In the north and in Ireland there is a single emergence in July to August. Most populations are small, with one or two hundred adults in summer and even fewer in the first (spring) brood. They flit just above the ground by day and roost communally by night on tall sheltered grass clumps, head down with two to five butterflies per stem. This makes a beautiful spectacle in early morning when they bask before dispersing.

Distribution and status

This is the commonest and most widely distributed of our Blue butterflies. Colonies are found throughout the British Isles and on many of the smaller and most northerly islands, where the females are particularly large, blue and beautiful. It is absent only from the north Shetlands and on mountains above 500 m.

Although still ubiquitous along all coasts, numerous inland colonies have been eliminated from flat regions due to the intensification of agriculture.

▨ confirmed range

CHALKHILL BLUE *Polyommatus coridon*

Adult identification
Average wingspan 38 mm

The large males are unmistakable both in flight and when basking, due to their cold, pale, silvery-blue upperwings. The underwings are also distinctive – heavily spotted on a light grey background that appears almost white in the sun.

▲ *A mating pair of Chalkhill Blues perch on round-headed rampion on a Hampshire nature reserve; only the male has milky blue upperwings.*

The females have chocolate-brown upperwings, tinged to a variable extent by silver-blue near the body. Elderly females overlap with the first Adonis Blues in late August and early September. They differ from female Adonis Blues in having white rather than blue outer circles to the eye spots along the bottom edges of the upper hindwings, and from all other Blues in having brown vein ends across the white fringes, making the edges look chequered.

Young stages
This butterfly hibernates as an **egg**, which is laid singly on the stems of horseshoe vetch or tough vegetation near to this plant. It is off-white and robust, and easily found from August to October, after which most drop to the ground where they spend the winter. Examine large mats of low-growing vetch.

The egg hatches in spring, and as it grows older, the **caterpillar** hides by day below the vetch but is easily spotted at dusk in early June when it surfaces

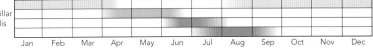

	Jan	Feb	Mar	Apr	May	Jun	Jul	Aug	Sep	Oct	Nov	Dec
egg												
caterpillar												
chrysalis												
adult												

(smothered by ants which protect it through most of its life in return for sugary secretions) to browse on horseshoe vetch leaves. It is very like the yellow-striped Adonis Blue caterpillar, which may be on the same plant in April and July.

The pale greenish **chrysalis** also produces sugary secretions and like any stationary sweet object is soon buried (and protected) by ants in earth cells. Nevertheless it is quite easily found in large colonies.

Habitat and behaviour

As its name implies, this beautiful butterfly is found on flower-rich chalk and limestone grassland, where the caterpillar's foodplant, horseshoe vetch (*Hippocrepis comosa*) grows abundantly. Most sites are exposed, south-facing slopes of steep downs or ancient earthworks, and there are many fine colonies in abandoned quarries. Unlike the Adonis Blue, which has the same foodplant, breeding can occur wherever horseshoe vetch grows. However the vetch itself needs fairly short or open conditions, at least for seedling establishment. Many Chalkhill Blue colonies declined and some were lost due to scrubbing up in the years following the death of rabbits by myxomatosis; even more have been destroyed by ploughing and agricultural improvement, which eliminates the vetch.

The adults fly in compact colonies, although individual males occasionally stray into unlikely habitats. Numbers fluctuate greatly; on the best sites it can be extraordinarily abundant, with tens of thousands of males flitting in a milky blue haze across the open downland. At night they roost in groups (page 17), often at the base of hills, head down and perched two or more to the stem on tall sheltered clumps of grass.

Distribution and status

Colonies are now restricted to the chalk and limestone downs of southern England, but once occurred as far north as Lincolnshire. Today, Cambridge, the Chilterns and Cotswolds mark the northern limit, and it is very local in all these areas, as well as in Somerset. Populations have largely been eliminated from the flatter chalklands of East Anglia, Salisbury Plain, and the south, but are still plentiful and to be expected on steep unimproved slopes in the southern counties, especially where the sward is short. Thus a string of colonies breed along the North Downs escarpment of Surrey and Kent, across the Dorset scarps and along the southern Dorset coast, and on the chalk hogsback straddling the Isle of Wight. Other colonies occur commonly on unfertilized south-facing slopes on the South Downs in Sussex, and in Hampshire and Wiltshire. Fortunately many fine colonies are safeguarded by nature reserves and agri-environment schemes.

 confirmed range

ADONIS BLUE *Polyommatus bellargus*

Adult identification

Average wingspan 38 mm

The male has brilliant upperwings of almost turquoise blue, and outer margins edged with a fine black line. The female upperwings are mainly chocolate-brown, but often dusted near the base with turquoise-blue, and have small black eye-

▲ *A male Adonis Blue sucking on mud for salts, revealing his brilliant blue upperwings with white fringes that are crossed by short black veins.*

spots within orange and blue surrounds along the lower margins. Dark veins cross the white fringes of the wing edges in both sexes, just entering the body of the wings. The underwings are spotted with orange near the edges. Many female Adonis and Chalkhill Blues are identical, except on the uppersides where the pupil between eye-spot and wing edge is blue on this species but white on the Chalkhill Blue (page 35). The Common Blue has no dark veins across its white fringes in either sex.

Young stages

The **egg** is a white disc with a faint pattern of radiating spikes. It is laid singly beneath the youngest leaflets of horse-shoe vetch. It is easy to find in September – examine unshaded plants growing flat against the ground in warm bare depressions or in pockets of very short turf. In June, a wider range of vetch growth-forms is used, making it harder to find.

The green and yellow **caterpillar** is beautifully camouflaged as it feeds by

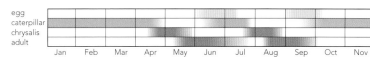

	Jan	Feb	Mar	Apr	May	Jun	Jul	Aug	Sep	Oct	Nov	Dec
egg												
caterpillar												
chrysalis												
adult												

day, exposed on tender horseshoe vetch leaves. It may be distinguished from the Chalkhill Blue by its daytime feeding and by the date, and from the Common Blue by its yellow stripes and lack of hairs. It can be found, quite easily, in April and late July by looking for agitated ants which invariably attend and 'milk' the caterpillar of sugary secretions. Young second-brood caterpillars hibernate on the foodplant in October.

The **chrysalis** is also attended by ants. It is formed underground either inside ant nests or in crevices, where it is soon earthed up by ants in a little cell. It is hard, but not impossible, to find on good sites.

Habitat and behaviour

The Adonis Blue lives in discrete colonies on the hottest parts of unfertilized chalk or limestone grasslands that contain the caterpillar's foodplant, horseshoe vetch (*Hippocrepis comosa*), in abundance. Typical sites are steep south-facing downs and ancient earthworks where the sward is so short or sparse that the sun bakes the ground during the autumn and spring caterpillar-feeding periods. Other sites are more overgrown, but support small colonies where breeding is restricted to a minority of vetch plants, for example along path edges. If sites cease to be grazed, they soon lose their colony: there was a spate of extinctions after rabbits disappeared from unfarmed downs in the 1950s, and a substantial recovery when they returned from the 1990s onwards, helped, no doubt, by the warmer springs.

Whatever their average size, colonies also fluctuate greatly from one year to another, and the summer emergence is usually more numerous than the spring one. Many colonies contain fewer than 100 adults, but after a warm summer, tens of thousands may be seen shimmering above the close-cropped turf of the best sites. Most will be males; the females fly less often and are inconspicuous.

Distribution and status

This is a scarce inhabitant of the warmest downs of southern England. It is locally common on steep downland in Dorset, Wiltshire and the Isle of Wight. Scattered colonies also breed along the escarpment of the North Downs in Surrey and Kent, on some Sussex downs, and, more locally, in Hampshire and the Chilterns. In the late 1970s it had become reduced to about 75 sites, but with the return of rabbits and sheep to abandoned downs there has been a considerable recovery; 35 years on, at least 300 sites now support this beautiful butterfly. In a few regions, such as the Cotswolds, the spread of this sedentary insect was hastened by the release of adults, but in most areas it resulted from an exceptional build-up of numbers on the existing sites.

confirmed range

HOLLY BLUE *Celastrina argiolus*

Adult identification

Average wingspan 35 mm

Any blue butterfly seen fluttering several feet up around shrubs, trees, along hedgerows or in gardens in southern Britain is likely to be a Holly Blue. This, however, is not a safe means of identifica-

▲ *A male Holly Blue in his normal perching position with the wings held half open. This Blue butterfly may be seen in gardens and parks even in central London.*

tion. The diagnostic feature in both sexes is the underwing, which is clear silver-blue with tiny black dots and no orange marks. It gives the Holly Blue a distinctly silver look in flight and makes it unmistakable at rest. Only the Small Blue is similar, but this is much smaller and has sooty upperwings. The upperwings of the Holly Blue are violet-blue; indeed the male resembles a male Common Blue from above. The female upperwings are more distinctive because they have wide dark borders and tips, especially in the second brood.

Young stages

The **egg** is a white disc that is laid singly and easily found on the flowers or flower buds of shrubs, mainly holly in springtime and ivy in the summer brood, although gorse, dogwood, spindle and other bushes may be used.

The **caterpillar** may be easily found among the berries of these plants, lying

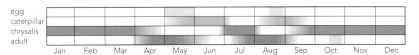

	Jan	Feb	Mar	Apr	May	Jun	Jul	Aug	Sep	Oct	Nov	Dec
egg												
caterpillar												
chrysalis												
adult												

over a fruit like a green slug, piercing the centre and sucking up the contents, leaving conspicuous feeding damage and droppings everywhere. When fully grown, it is pale translucent green, sometimes with purple or rose marks on the flanks and a yellow or white line down the back.

The **chrysalis** is dark brown and formed in a crevice or on the ground, where it is almost impossible to find.

Habitat and behaviour

This attractive little butterfly differs from our other Blues in two respects. First, it is quite mobile: although more or less resident colonies may persist for years in certain woods and parks, the adults also roam over wide areas of town and countryside, laying eggs at low densities wherever suitable breeding sites are encountered. The other difference is that it breeds on shrubs rather than low-growing vetches and herbs. The fruit of holly (*Ilex aquifolium*) in spring, ivy (*Hedera helix*) in summer, as well as gorse (*Ulex* spp.), dogwood (*Thelycrania sanguinea*), spindle (*Euonymus europaeus*) and alder buckthorn (*Frangula alnus*) in season. Thus, this butterfly is typically seen in ones or twos, anywhere within its range, in gardens, along hedgerows and, especially, in woods. It often breeds in towns, including central London. Other Blues live in compact colonies in open grassland.

Holly Blue numbers vary greatly over the years, booming and busting in roughly seven-year cycles. But whatever the year, numbers are usually higher in the second (August) brood. There are two generations of adults in most years, but often just one, in midsummer, in Ireland. In England it is the earliest Blue to emerge, having hibernated as a chrysalis.

Search for adults from April onwards, and again in late July and August. It may be seen fluttering high up among shrubs and trees and rarely settles on the ground. It often rests on bushes, usually with the wings closed or half open, so that the silver underwings are visible.

Distribution and status

The Holly Blue may be seen throughout much of England, but is commonest in the south and at low altitudes. In peak years it is common over this whole area, and individuals are seen around suitable shrubs almost anywhere. In other years it is virtually absent, apparently due to a build-up of a beautiful parasitic wasp that kills many caterpillars. If anything, it has increased slightly in recent years, especially in northern England. It is much more localized in Wales, restricted largely to the lowlands. Its distribution in Ireland is also sparse, and largely confined to coastal regions, especially in the south and east.

confirmed range

LARGE BLUE *Maculinea arion*

Adult identification

Average wingspan: 38 mm (♂) to 44 mm (♀); occasionally 25 mm miniatures

The upperwings of both sexes of this rare butterfly have broad black borders, with four to six black spots on the

▲ *A female Large Blue basks on a Somerset nature reserve. The wings are opened only in weak sunlight. See page 4 for underside.*

forewings, although the black is often reduced on males. The undersides range from silver to fawn, with black spots but no orange marks, and a dusting of bright turquoise near the body. Flight is weak and fluttery compared with other Blues, giving an inky blue-black image that can be confused with a female Holly Blue. Male Common Blues also look similar in flight, but are more violet and darting – if in any doubt, it is unlikely that you have seen a Large Blue.

Young stages

The **egg** is a white disc, and easy to find by gently parting the largest flowerheads of wild thyme in late June. Note that a licence is required before searching for them.

The young **caterpillar** is brownish-pink, and first bores into a thyme floret. It is easier to find three weeks later in July, beautifully camouflaged but living openly on the flowerhead. It then deserts its

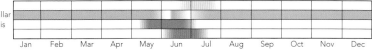

	Jan	Feb	Mar	Apr	May	Jun	Jul	Aug	Sep	Oct	Nov	Dec
egg												
caterpillar												
chrysalis												
adult												

flower and is carried into a red ant nest, where it lives for ten months feeding on ant brood. The maggot-like white caterpillar lives quite deep in the nest and is almost never found by turning stones.

The **chrysalis** is pale brown and lives in the chambers of its host ant nest.

Habitat and behaviour
Due to its extraordinary life-cycle, which requires high densities of wild thyme (*Thymus praecox*) and *Myrmica sabuleti* red ants to co-exist on the same site, this large and beautiful Blue has always been one of our rarest butterflies. In Britain it inhabits unfertilized grassland where the soil is exceptionally warm and well drained, but at the same time not prone to drought. Nearly all sites are sheltered south-facing hillsides that are grazed very short in spring and autumn, allowing the soil to warm up during the key growth periods of its food, *Myrmica* ant grubs. Those in Devon and Cornwall are on acidic shales and schists, where gorse and heather grow among the sward; those in Somerset and the Cotswolds are limestone grasslands.

Like most Blues, this is a colonial species that seldom strays from its breeding areas. As a predator, the Large Blue forms smaller colonies than its plant-eating relatives, each typically containing a few tens of adults. However on some nature reserves, ideal management has generated populations of several thousand adults, making an unforgettable sight as their slate-blue wings hover and jink above the thyme-scented turf. They are especially active in the morning.

Distribution and status
The Large Blue has always been a great rarity, confined to six regions in central and south-west England. By the early 1900s it was reduced to three areas, and after the mid-1950s its 30 surviving colonies suffered a steeper decline, the last becoming extinct in 1979. By then its ecology was just understood, and in 1983 a near-identical race from Sweden was successfully re-established on a carefully managed former site on the edge of Dartmoor. Since then its habitat has been restored in five former regions, and further introductions were made in the early 1990s. By 2013 the Large Blue was established in growing numbers on two sites in the Cotswolds, but its stronghold is in the Polden Hills, Somerset. There the butterfly has spread to more than 30 sites, some supporting large populations. Few have public access, but the National Trust and Somerset Wildlife Trust hold open weekends in most years. There is also a fine colony on Collard Down, near Street, with parking and public access throughout the flight period: see the NT's and SWT's websites for details.

confirmed
range

DUKE OF BURGUNDY *Hamearis lucina*

Adult identification

Average wingspan 29 mm (♂) to 32 mm (♀)

This little butterfly is the size and shape of a Blue, but has the markings of a Fritillary, and is the only European member of the vast Metalmark family of butterflies. Its upperwings are blackish-brown with pale orange patches in the outer half, and black spots round the edges of all

▲ *A view of the little Duke of Burgundy, perched with wings half open on a large cowslip leaf.*

wings. The under forewing is similar, but lighter, whilst the under hindwing has two conspicuous bands of white cells, a third and two-thirds out from the body.

All our Fritillaries (pages 40–42), except occasionally the Marsh, are larger and none has a double band of white on the under hindwing nor spots round every wing edge. In flight it can resemble the day-flying Latticed Heath moth, a very dark Small Copper (page 33) and, even more, the rare Chequered Skipper (page 46). Note that the latter has a broad head and body, huge eyes, no black spots, and an irregular pattern of white cells on the under hindwing.

Young stages

The **egg** is laid in small groups of two to five beneath cowslip and primrose leaves. Each is spherical with a glassy transparent shell through which the creamy contents and, later, the caterpillar's dark hairs are clearly visible. Eggs are easy to find on suitable *Primula* (see Habitat) early in June, but note that fresh eggs resemble those of some moths.

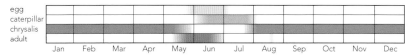

	Jan	Feb	Mar	Apr	May	Jun	Jul	Aug	Sep	Oct	Nov	Dec
egg												
caterpillar												
chrysalis												
adult												

The **caterpillar** is hairy and, when young, can easily be found resting under a *Primula* leaf that has obvious perforations, although note that slugs and moth caterpillars cause similar damage. When older it is long, flat, grey-brown, and very hairy, and lives in the leaf litter beneath its plant, emerging to eat leaves at night.

The **chrysalis** hibernates inconspicuously among dead leaves. It is beautifully marked with black spots on a cream background, and has fine hairs.

Habitat and behaviour

The Duke of Burgundy lives in small close-knit colonies in only a few of the places where *Primula* grow. Typical sites are warm pockets of grassland among scrub on chalk and limestone hills, and sunny sheltered rides, glades, or recent clearings in woodland, where the ground flora is beginning to grow up. In both situations, eggs are laid on large leaved cowslips (*Primula veris*) or primroses (*P. vulgaris*) growing quite prominently in warm spots, sheltered and half-shaded beneath shrubs, along ditches, or on the edge of denser woodland. Small exposed *Primula* growing in open grassland are rejected, as are heavily shaded plants. On many sites this represents a transitional habitat which exists for a few years following a clearing. Within woods, colonies shift as clearings become shaded and new ones are formed. However, they seldom move far and, by and large, this is a remarkably sedentary butterfly.

Most colonies are confined to very small areas and contain a few tens of adults, so the butterfly is usually seen in ones and twos. The male is easy to find, for he will perch with wings open on a prominent grass clump or twig, at the edge of a clearing or where woodland rides meet. Any passing butterfly is intercepted in a rapid buzzing flight, female Duke of Burgundies being pursued vigorously after which the male will return to his original perch.

Distribution and status

The Duke of Burgundy was once locally common in sunny woods over much of southern England, and also bred in Wales and as far north as south Scotland. Few woods are unshaded enough to support a colony any longer, and it is now one of our most rapidly declining species. Probably fewer than 100 colonies survive, mainly in scrubby grassland, but many are small and threatened. The current strongholds are on the chalk of Wiltshire and Hampshire, followed by the Sussex downs and Cotswolds, with smaller pockets in Dorset, Somerset and the Chilterns. Although extinct in Wales and East Anglia, it survives in three areas farther north: around Peterborough, in North Yorkshire, and in the Lake District.

▨ confirmed range

WHITE ADMIRAL *Limenitis camilla*

Adult identification

Average wingspan 60 mm (♂) to 64 mm (♀)

Both sexes of this elegant woodland butterfly look similar, apart from the male's smaller size and slightly darker colour. The upperwings are dusky brown – almost black on young males – with a conspic-

young caterpillar

▲ *The White Admiral is a common sight feeding on bramble in large southern woods.*

uous white band across both wings. The underwings have the same pattern, with an extra white area near the body and a lighter, more intricate bronze background adorned with black stripes and spots. Seen close up, no British species looks similar, and the black and white wing pattern is also distinctive in flight. Be warned, however, that hopeful entomologists often mistake an adult silhouetted high in the sky for the Purple Emperor (page 114). The White Admiral is much smaller, with more rounded wings and a daintier flight.

Young stages

The **egg** is laid singly and looks like a miniature sea urchin – round and grey with a honeycomb of ridges over the surface, and numerous fine translucent spines. It is quite easy to find on the upper edges of the leaves of suitable honeysuckles (see Habitat).

In August the spiny brown young **caterpillar** is ridiculously easy to locate, although minute, due to the conspicuous

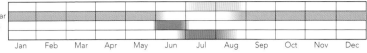

	Jan	Feb	Mar	Apr	May	Jun	Jul	Aug	Sep	Oct	Nov	Dec
egg												
caterpillar												
chrysalis												
adult												

feeding damage. By nibbling the leaf blade back from the tip in a line at right angles to the midrib, it leaves the midrib intact and protruding, and rests on the tip of this. In September it folds the remains of a leaf double with silk cords to hibernate inside. This tent soon withers, but remains and can be found by patient searching during winter, as can the growing caterpillar in spring. When fully grown, it is bright green with red-brown spines. Its presence is often betrayed by seeping, nibbled leaves.

The **chrysalis** is as beautiful as the caterpillar. Green and purple with silver points, it has a curious outline including two 'ears' on the head and a prominent knob halfway up. It hangs among honeysuckle looking like a half-dead, rolled leaf, but with practice can be found.

Habitat and behaviour

The White Admiral is a creature of extensive woodlands. Thin spindly growths of honeysuckle (*Lonicera periclymenum*) are chosen for breeding: examine wisps dangling in dappled sunlight beneath boughs, and half-shaded plants overhanging ditches or scrambling weakly amongst trees beside a ride. Vigorous bushy plants with abundant flowers, sprawling in sunny clearings or over hedgerows, are never used. Thus quite shady woods are the habitat of this butterfly, such as abandoned coppices and deciduous forests where the canopy has almost closed. Small populations breed along the ride edges of conifer plantations, but are shaded out as these mature into gloomy plots.

Unlike its young stages, the adult is rather elusive and generally seen in ones and twos. Long periods are spent basking and drinking aphid honeydew, hidden from view in the forest canopy. It has a swift, elegant flight of short flits and long glides, soaring high into the sky then rapidly down, hugging the contours of the canopy.

Distribution and status

This is a local butterfly that just penetrates south-east Wales, but is otherwise confined to England south of the Humber. Its stronghold is in the southern central counties of Dorset, Hampshire, Sussex, Surrey, Wiltshire, Berkshire, Buckinghamshire and Oxford, where it is locally common – but seldom abundant – in some small woods, many large ones, and can be expected in major woodland complexes such as those of the West Weald and New Forest. It is much rarer around the fringes of this area, in Somerset, Devon, the Kent Weald, Gloucestershire and the East Midlands forest belt up to Peterborough and beyond. Despite a recent spread in East Anglia and Lincolnshire, many colonies have disappeared in recent years within its former range, and overall this is a species in worrying decline.

■■■ confirmed
range

PURPLE EMPEROR *Apatura iris*

Adult identification

Average wingspan 75 mm (♂) to 84 mm (♀)

Both sexes of this particularly large woodland butterfly look similar, except in sunshine when, at certain angles, the

▲ *The male Purple Emperor's wings appear purple like this only when they catch the sun.*

male's upperwings refract the light and turn brilliant iridescent purple. At all other times the background colour is dusky, with a solid white band across the hindwings and patches of white on the forewings. The underwings have the same white markings as the upperwings, but the background colour is a beautiful blurred mixture of grey, pink, red-brown and silver – very different from the neat pattern on the White Admiral, the only butterfly with which it can be confused (page 112).

Young stages

The **egg** is as readily found as the adult, although neither is very easy. Search the upper surfaces of suitable sallow leaves in August. It is dome-shaped with 14 vertical ribs, about 1 mm high, and glossy green when fresh but soon developing a conspicuous purple band.

The **caterpillar** is delightfully camouflaged. After the first moult it is 9 mm

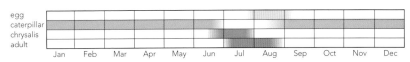

	Jan	Feb	Mar	Apr	May	Jun	Jul	Aug	Sep	Oct	Nov	Dec
egg												
caterpillar												
chrysalis												
adult												

long, grey-brown, with two horns on the head. It hibernates on a silk pad in the fork or crotch of a sallow twig, and can be found by patient searching during winter. The fully grown green caterpillar is less often seen (page 7). It sits on silk on a sallow leaf by day, and roams over the bush at night, feeding on leaves before returning to its silk pad.

The **chrysalis** hangs beneath a sallow leaf where its pale silver-green colour makes it almost impossible to find.

Habitat and behaviour

The Purple Emperor is confined to large forests and to extensively wooded regions where numerous copses and spinneys lie between more substantial woods. It is commonest on heavy soils where the shrub layer contains an abundance of the caterpillar's foodplants – broad- and narrow-leaved sallows (*Salix caprea* and *S. cinerea*). Fairly prominent, medium- to large-sized bushes growing in nooks or beside glades and rides are chosen. The eggs are laid singly on partly shaded leaves within the crown or body of the bush.

This is one of our least conspicuous butterflies. It lives in more or less compact colonies, each colony breeding at low densities over a wide area and usually encompassing several woods. Males congregate on the canopy of a tall tree in one wood, usually on a high point, where they perch and make spectacular soaring flights and battle with each other flashing purple as they catch the sun. The same 'master tree' is used year after year, and this is the place to see this beautiful butterfly at its best. Males descend occasionally to drink at puddles or sap, but feed mainly on aphid honeydew on the tree-tops. The females are seldom seen. After briefly visiting the master tree to mate, they disperse to fly rapidly among shaded branches in search of suitable sallows, which they enter and promptly disappear.

Distribution and status

Although scarce, the Purple Emperor is often overlooked and is not quite as rare as is popularly supposed. It once bred in most of the heavily wooded districts of Wales and England south of the Humber, but is now largely confined to central southern English counties. Its stronghold is the heavily wooded Wealden Clays of west Surrey and Sussex, where it probably breeds in most copses and woods, extending on to the sandstones and well into Hampshire. There are strong concentrations elsewhere in Hampshire, but very low numbers in the New Forest. Its other main centres are south Wiltshire, and the Buckinghamshire/north-east Oxfordshire border. Rare colonies are believed to survive in Dorset, Somerset, Devon, Gloucestershire, Nottinghamshire and East Anglia; not all have been mapped.

▓ confirmed
range

Adult identification

Average wingspan 67 mm (♂) to 72 mm (♀)

The Red Admiral is one of Britain's largest and most vividly marked butterflies, and is unmistakable whether settled or in flight. The males are slightly smaller but both sexes look similar. When not flying, it usually basks with its wings wide open, exposing soft velvet black upper-

tent

▲ *The magnificent Red Admiral is a regular visitor to gardens throughout the British Isles for much of the summer and autumn.*

wings with a brilliant band of scarlet diagonally across each forewing and round the bottom edge of each hindwing. The top corner of the forewing contains striking white patches, and there is a series of black spots in the lower band of scarlet, with a blue patch at the bottom.

The underside of the forewing is a duller version of the uppersides, and is generally quite conspicuous. However, when roosting, it is pulled down between the underwings so that only its dark tip is visible. The underwings are then camouflaged to resemble dark bark in shades of mottled brown, grey and black.

Young stages

The **egg** is laid singly and can be found on the upper surface of small young leaves of stinging nettles or, occasionally hop. It is 0.8 mm high, and oblong, with eight to ten (usually nine) prominent glassy ridges running from top to bottom. Although pale green at first, it blackens as the embryo develops.

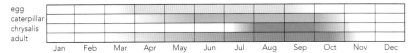

	Jan	Feb	Mar	Apr	May	Jun	Jul	Aug	Sep	Oct	Nov	Dec
egg												
caterpillar												
chrysalis												
adult												

The **caterpillar** feeds on nettle leaves and lives hidden in a tent of one or several leaves, folded over and fastened together by silk. This is quite easy to find in July and early September. Inside, the caterpillar sits coiled in a figure of '6' shape. When fully grown (35 mm long) it is plump, spiny and very variable in colour – anything from dark, light or olive-brown, with tiny white speckles. There is a broad band of yellow along each side, often broken into patches.

The **chrysalis** hangs suspended inside the caterpillar's last tent. It is pale grey with gold points.

Habitat and behaviour

The Red Admiral may be seen in any habitat and at all altitudes throughout the British Isles, but is commonest around woods, gardens, orchards and hedgerows, where there is shelter and an abundance of flowers. It is a migratory species that is unable to survive the British winter except in very small numbers. Happily, each year adults teem northwards from the Mediterranean, rapidly spreading through Europe and always reaching Britain and Ireland. They are powerful fliers, alternating between strong wing flits and elegant glides.

The males establish territories along warm edges, such as hedgerows, each patrolling the same area day after day. After mating, the females search for nettles (*Urtica* spp.) or rarely hop, flitting rapidly between plants and generally choosing those that are growing in full sunshine for egg-laying – large nettle beds and isolated plants are both used. By late summer feeding becomes a preoccupation, and both sexes are attracted to warm sheltered places containing flowers, such as gardens. They have a penchant for the juices of rotting fruit and sap from injured trees, and will gather and jostle in orchards and woods for these delights. As the nights get colder, there is good evidence of a return migration to the continent, but some try to hibernate in quite exposed places, and almost invariably perish.

Distribution and status

Red Admirals arrive in variable numbers from late May onwards and spread throughout the British Isles reaching all our larger islands, including the Shetlands, every year. Even the remotest places such as the central Highlands of Scotland are colonized. Peak numbers are reached one or two broods later, in September, when it is usually a common, although seldom abundant, butterfly of flowery, sheltered habitats and gardens everywhere. Despite considerable fluctuations from year to year, the trend in recent years has been a gradual increase, probably reflecting the warmer weather over Europe and perhaps the spread of lush nitrogen-rich nettles in our heavily farmed countryside.

maximum range

PAINTED LADY *Vanessa cardui*

Adult identification

Average wingspan 64 mm (♂) to 70 mm (♀)

The Painted Lady usually settles with its wings wide open, displaying a chequered pattern of black veins, spots and patches against a background that varies from pale salmon-pink to dull orange. As in the Red Admiral (page 116), there is a small patch of blue on the bottom corner of each hindwing, and the apex of the forewing is black with shining white markings.

▲ *The Painted Lady is usually seen in open habitats where there is an abundance of flowers for it to feed upon.*

The underside of the forewing is a very pale version of its upperside, but the under hindwing is quite different. It has a mottled and intricate pattern of brown, grey, white and blue, with small and slightly fuzzy blue, black and yellow eyespots (page 38).

No other European butterfly is similar to the Painted Lady. It is the palest and pinkest of all Nymphalids, and appears especially so when flying.

Young stages

The **egg** is laid singly on the uppersides of thistle leaves and other foodplants, and can be found quite easily in places where the adult has been seen. It is small (0.6 mm high), oval, with 16 prominent glassy ridges running from top to bottom. When laid it is light green, but turns silver-grey as it develops.

The **caterpillar** crawls under its egg-leaf and spins a fine web in which it hides, eating the underside of the (usually thistle) leaf and leaving distinctive patches of shining outer cuticle that are easy to find. It eventually eats the whole leaf except the spines, and later spins a tent

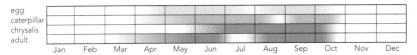

	Jan	Feb	Mar	Apr	May	Jun	Jul	Aug	Sep	Oct	Nov	Dec
egg												
caterpillar												
chrysalis												
adult												

of leaves in which it lives and feeds, becoming increasingly conspicuous as droppings collect in the silk. These tents are easy to find in late June and early July. The caterpillar inside is about 30 mm long, black and spiny, with a broken stripe of bright yellow down each side, and a rather square-cut head.

The **caterpillar** often moves and forms a new tent of thistle leaves where the chrysalis develops. This is greyish-pink, delicately burnished with gold, and very beautiful.

Habitat and behaviour

The Painted Lady is a migratory butterfly that may be found, in most years, in any sunny open habitat. It is unable to hibernate and hardly ever survives the British winter. Our populations originate from north or even sub-Saharan Africa, where numbers build up each spring leading to annual outbreaks. The adult has a powerful gliding flight, and it is one of the great sights of entomology to see them swarming in countless thousands across the Mediterranean and northwards over Europe, eventually settling where the prevailing winds have driven them.

Migrant Painted Ladies sometimes reach Britain in February to April, but there is a regular, erratic influx from early June onwards. Individual males soon establish territories on sunny patches of ground a few yards wide in the shelter of hedges, woods and gardens. They bask on the warm earth and periodically make short rapid flights around their beats. When mated, the females seek thistles (*Cirsium* spp. and *Carduus*.) or, less often, mallows or nettles for egg-laying, flying rapidly between exposed plants, often in cultivated fields. When numbers reach their peak in late summer, adults are seen in all habitats where there are flowers, including gardens, but especially in open warm places such as downs, heaths, dunes, and along the coastline.

Distribution and status

The abundance and range of the Painted Lady varies greatly from one year to the next, depending on the arrival of immigrants and their subsequent success in breeding. In most years they are commonest in the south, but prevailing winds occasionally drive early swarms of immigrants further north, where they breed in large numbers. There is probably no year when a few do not arrive in Britain, and in typical seasons they are encountered, but not necessarily expected, in ones or twos in flowery habitats throughout late summer and autumn. Every few years we have very large influxes, and then the Painted Lady becomes a common sight throughout the British Isles in all habitats up to the Shetlands. A return migration occurs in autumn, often at high altitude.

▨ maximum range

SMALL TORTOISESHELL *Aglais urticae*

Adult identification

Average wingspan 50 mm (♂) to 56 mm (♀)

Both sexes of this familiar butterfly look similar. It basks with the wings wide open, displaying bright reddish-orange uppersides with a dark border containing blue crescents around all outer edges. Six black patches break up the orange of each forewing, and there is a

▲ *The Small Tortoiseshell is one of our commonest butterflies and can often be seen basking on bramble.*

white spot near the outer tip. On the upper hindwing, a large area near the body is black, although obscured by orange hairs.

The underwings are sombre and camouflaged to resemble bark. They have a bluish-black inner half followed by a broad indistinct pale band, merging into a blue-black outer margin. The pale area is larger and the pattern more mottled on the under forewing.

No other species in Britain or Europe is likely to be confused with this common butterfly except the extremely rare Large Tortoiseshell (page 37).

Young stages

The **eggs** are laid in large clusters of 80–200, often several layers deep under tender leaves on young stinging nettle clumps. Each egg is globular and pale glassy-green, with eight or nine prominent ribs running from top to bottom. Batches are easy to find on suitable nettles (see Habitat), but note the similarities with the Peacock (page 124).

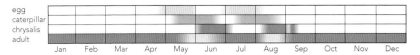

	Jan	Feb	Mar	Apr	May	Jun	Jul	Aug	Sep	Oct	Nov	Dec
egg												
caterpillar												
chrysalis												
adult												

Young **caterpillars** live gregariously on white silk webs spun over growths of nettle, splitting into smaller groups of 50–100 as they grow. They are extremely conspicuous, pale at first but becoming darker in later stages. In the final period they live separately, but are still easily found. They reach 22 mm in length, are spiny, and vary greatly in colour from yellow with black speckles to mainly black with yellow-based spines. See page 124 for the differences of the Peacock. Caterpillars scatter to pupate singly on vegetation or walls, where they are occasionally encountered.

The **chrysalis** varies in colour from lilac-pink washed with copper to dull smoke-brown.

Habitat and behaviour

This is a mobile butterfly that does not live in identifiable colonies, but flies freely across the countryside and even out to sea, occasionally reaching France. It may be seen in any habitat, but especially where flowers or common and annual 'stinging' nettles (*Urtica dioica* and *U. urens*) – the caterpillar's food – are abundant. Depending on the needs of the moment, it is commoner in some habitats than in others at certain times of year.

In early spring, adults emerge from hibernation and are mostly seen in sunny situations in the open countryside. The males bask and feed in the morning, then set up territories near nettlebeds in early afternoon, lying in wait for virgin females. Mating occurs deep among nettles and is rarely seen. Then the female leaves to find a suitable patch for egg-laying: young clumps of nettle growing in warm sheltered hollows are preferred, including those in the middle of fields. The next (summer) brood of adults behaves similarly, but their offspring, in August, do little else but feed in preparation for winter hibernation. These gather wherever there are flowers, and are very often attracted to gardens (page 22). Hibernation is also often near buildings; in garages, lofts, outhouses, cool rooms, and churches. In the north there may be a single emergence each year in July which survives to the following June.

Distribution and status

The Small Tortoiseshell is one of our commonest butterflies and may be expected, in season, wherever there are flowers or nettles anywhere in the British Isles. It is equally numerous on all soil types, reaching the highest mountain tops and our remotest islands, including the Shetlands. However, although ubiquitous and common, it is seldom seen in huge numbers at one time, as occurs with our more colonial butterflies.

Small Tortoiseshells are as common and widespread throughout Europe as they are in Britain.

███ confirmed range

LARGE TORTOISESHELL *Aglais polychloros*

Adult identification

Average wingspan 64 mm (♂) to 70 mm (♀)

Both sexes of this probably extinct butterfly look similar and, superficially, rather like the Small Tortoiseshell (page

young caterpillars

▲ *The Large Tortoiseshell is probably extinct as a resident species, but adults from the continent are frequently released.*

120). Note the duller orange upperwings of the Large Tortoiseshell, its larger size, the much smaller area of black on the upper hindwing, and that there is an extra black spot but no white patch on the upper forewing. In addition, this species almost never has blue spots along the outer edge of the upper forewing, unlike the Small Tortoiseshell which always does.

The under hindwings look like pale bark, with no sharp pattern. Hairs project from the forewing. In flight, Commas and male Silver-washed Fritillaries are occasionally mistaken for this butterfly.

Young stages

The **eggs** are laid in batches of about 200 forming a sleeve round the slender terminal twigs of tall elms and other trees (see Habitat). They are inaccessible high up in the elm canopy and, being pale

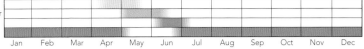

	Jan	Feb	Mar	Apr	May	Jun	Jul	Aug	Sep	Oct	Nov	Dec
egg												
caterpillar												
chrysalis												
adult												

brown, are hard to see. Each is conical, with seven to nine (usually eight) prominent vertical ridges.

The **caterpillars** live gregariously for their whole lives, resting on conspicuous webs spun over twigs and browsing the leaves beneath them. When fully grown, each is velvety black with amber bristles, stripes, white dots and fine hairs, giving a greyish impression overall. It drops to the ground (often from a treetop) to pupate solitarily on a shrub or another tree.

The **chrysalis** is pale brown with gold spots, and looks so like a dead leaf it is very difficult to find.

Habitat and behaviour

During the second half of the 20th century, the Large Tortoiseshell was a rare butterfly that did not live in stable colonies, but roamed the countryside and was generally seen in ones or twos. Despite this, certain wooded districts were occupied for several successive broods, allowing numbers to build up to local abundance before inexplicably disappearing again for some years. Typical sites were forest edges, avenues, and wooded lanes where clumps of elm (*Ulmus* spp.) were common. There is little doubt that elms were the preferred foodplant, although caterpillars have also been found on sallows, willows, aspen, poplar, birch, whitethorn, pear and cherry.

The adults emerged in high summer to feed briefly before hibernating in hollow trees, wood piles, and sheltered spots. The following March they re-emerged and could be seen feeding on pussy willows or basking with wings held wide open against warm patches of bare ground. At other times they rarely settled, but flew backwards and forwards among the treetops with a powerful gliding flight punctuated by short rapid wingbeats.

Distribution and status

This lovely Nymphalid is probably extinct as a resident butterfly in Britain, and there is now no place where one can guarantee or even hope to see it today. A few genuine sightings (and many more misidentifications) are still made each year, especially in the Isle of Wight, which is the most likely candidate for a residual native population, albeit a very small one. Most accurate records, however, are almost certainly of captive stock that has escaped or been released by entomologists who regularly return with caterpillars from France where 'nests' are still quite easy to find. Whatever the source, most sightings are made in southern England, with a few in Wales, fewer still in Scotland, and none in Ireland.

The last period of comparative abundance for this butterfly was the late 1940s. Periods of extreme scarcity have occurred in the past, but the last 65 years has been an unprecedented time of low numbers, with the more recent loss of many elms hardly encouraging its recovery.

presumed extinct
(records for last
200 years)

PEACOCK *Inachis io*

Adult identification

Average wingspan 63 mm (♂) to 69 mm (♀)

This spectacular large butterfly is one of the easiest to identify. The wings have scalloped edges and are often opened, revealing a background colour of deep chestnut with broad smoky-grey borders. Dominating each hindwing is the unmistakable 'peacock eye' – glossy blue and black within a fuzzy halo of white. There is

▲ One of our larger more common butterflies is the magnificent Peacock. Here a female basks on bramble, a favourite nectar source for many butterflies in summer.

also an 'eye' on each forewing, but this is blurred and of mixed colours, as if painted in abstract.

The underwings make a stark contrast, for they are beautifully camouflaged to resemble tree bark. Grey-black, with a steely blue sheen, black wavy lines and prominent black veins, they are darker and less patterned than the underwings of any related species. An old Peacock seen flying in spring may sometimes be mistaken for the Small Tortoiseshell; note that the latter has a weaker, more whirring wingbeat.

young caterpillars

Young stages

The **eggs** are laid in batches of up to 500, often six deep beneath tender leaves of stinging nettles. Each is pale green and oblong, with eight prominent ridges (looking like fluted glass) running from top to bottom. Batches can be found in early July on the particular nettles used for egg-laying (see Habitat). Note that the Small Tortoiseshell's eggs are similar, but are found in May or late July.

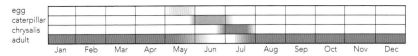

	Jan	Feb	Mar	Apr	May	Jun	Jul	Aug	Sep	Oct	Nov	Dec
egg												
caterpillar												
chrysalis												
adult												

The **caterpillars** are gregarious and extremely conspicuous basking on dense webs of silk spun over nettle leaves; nearby leaves are reduced to skeletons. The youngest caterpillars are grey-green, becoming darker at each moult until finally they are velvety black studded with tiny white warts and adorned with shining black forked spines. Over 40 mm long, they are larger and much darker than those of the gregarious Small Tortoiseshell, which are also conspicuous on nettles. Fully grown Peacock caterpillars scatter to pupate separately in distant vegetation or high up in trees.

The **chrysalis** is yellow-green with pink and gold points.

Habitat and behaviour

Peacock butterflies do not live in strict colonies, but fly freely and powerfully through the countryside, feeding and breeding wherever suitable conditions are encountered. They turn up in most habitats, depending on the season and their activity, but are always commonest in and around woods.

On emerging in July, fresh adults are preoccupied with feeding before settling down to winter hibernation. This takes them into gardens (page 22) and other flowery places, where they are a familiar sight in high summer; woodland rides containing teasels also attract scores of Peacocks. Hibernation occurs mainly in woods, often inside hollow trees where large numbers may congregate. The following spring, males establish separate territories along wood edges and bushy hedgerows, which the females visit for mating. Egg-laying occurs along the same sheltered edges, on large tall clumps of stinging nettle (*Urtica dioica*) which catch the sun around midday, when the eggs are laid. Thus, for most of its activities, the Peacock is much more closely connected with woodland than is the Small Tortoiseshell. Although one brood of adults a year is usual, emerging in July and lasting until the following spring, after warm summers there may be a small second emergence of autumn adults in the south.

Distribution and status

The Peacock is a common resident throughout most of England, Wales and Ireland, and its large southern populations are reinforced by migrants from the continent in some years. Numbers have increased everywhere during the past 40 years, and it has spread across the north of Ireland and England, and to a lesser extent in the Welsh uplands, where breeding sites are less common. A similar expansion has occurred in Scotland, where it is now resident across a broad band of the south: occasional migrating individuals may be seen much farther afield, even in the Shetlands.

confirmed range

COMMA *Polygonia c-album*

Adult identification

Average wingspan 55 mm (♂) to 60 mm (♀)

This is our only butterfly with really jagged edges to its wings. When they are closed, the Comma looks like a dead leaf with a distinctive white comma mark on the hindwing, which gives this butterfly its name (page 37).

▲ *This female Comma has lighter, less ragged wings than the male.*

The upperwings are orange with brown and black blotches and a dark edge to the ragged outline. In the midsummer emergence, up to one-third of the adults are of a form called *hutchinsoni*, which has faint markings and is brighter and more golden, with less ragged wing edges.

No other British butterfly is remotely similar when seen close-up, although flying adults, and *hutchinsoni* in particular, may be mistaken for Fritillaries.

Young stages

The **egg** is laid singly on the upper edges or tip of tender hop, nettle or elm leaves, and is quite easy to find in sunny pockets along wood edges and hedgerows. It is glassy green and nearly spherical, with ten or eleven prominent white ridges running from top to bottom.

The **caterpillar** lives beneath, and later on top of its leaf, and is as remarkably camouflaged in its own unsavoury way as the adult – it resembles a bird dropping. When small it is dark brown and crusty

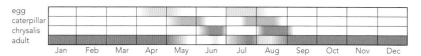

	Jan	Feb	Mar	Apr	May	Jun	Jul	Aug	Sep	Oct	Nov	Dec
egg												
caterpillar												
chrysalis												
adult												

with white patches, but when fully grown it is spiny and tan-coloured, with a splash of pure white down most of the back. Once this camouflage is known, the caterpillar is easy to find.

The **chrysalis** is shaped like an upside-down sea horse, and is a beautiful pinkish-brown with silver and gold marks. It hangs deep among vegetation and is almost impossible to find.

Habitat and behaviour

The Comma is less migratory than the Peacock and other close relatives, but is fairly mobile and does not live in identifiable colonies. Within a parish it flies between different sites to feed and breed, and is usually seen in ones or twos. Typical habitats are woods, copses, tall hedges, hedged lanes, scrubby corners and mature gardens.

The adults hibernate in woods, and next spring males establish well-separated territories, each in a glade or sunny nook along a wood edge, ride or sheltered hedge. He perches on a prominent leaf, leaving to intercept any passing butterfly in a swift gliding flight before returning to the original leaf; passing Comma females are pursued and courted. After mating the females search for hop (*Humulus lupulus*), nettles (*Urtica* spp.) and elm (*Ulmus* spp.) for egg-laying, but choose those plants growing along sunny rides, woodland edges, or sheltered hedges.

Springtime adults look normal, but the first that emerge in midsummer (July/August) are *hutchinsoni*. These behave similarly to the spring Commas and hence are seen mainly around woods. The slightly later emerging mid-summer adults are of the normal type and do not breed until next year. Instead they prepare for hibernation by feeding voraciously on flowers, often in gardens. The offspring of the *hutchinsoni* emerge in September, and also look normal and fly to garden, hedgerow and woodland flowers before hibernating.

Distribution and status

The Comma has fluctuated in range and abundance over the past two centuries. In the early 19th century it was locally common and widespread in Wales and England, though scarce in the north. It then declined to become one of Britain's rarest butterflies from the mid-19th century to about 1910. Then a gradual recovery took place, which accelerated greatly during the past 40 years, making the Comma Britain's most rapidly increasing butterfly.

Today the Comma is a locally common butterfly, to be expected in wooded neighbourhoods throughout all English and Welsh counties, except at high altitudes. It recently crossed the border into south-east Scotland.

■ confirmed range

Adult identification

Average wingspan 41 mm (♂) to 44 mm (♀)

Features that distinguish this from other small Fritillaries are illustrated on pages 40–41 and described under the very similar Pearl-bordered Fritillary (page 130). In addition, note that its size is similar to the Pearl-bordered Fritillary, and that their occurrence overlaps for at

▲ *The Small Pearl-bordered Fritillary has highly distinctive underwings with a complex pattern of silver, pale yellow and red-brown patches.*

least a fortnight in early June. The upperwings of this butterfly are, on average, brighter and more richly coloured than on the Pearl-bordered Fritillary and the black is darker and glossier. In the west, female Small Pearl-bordered Fritillaries often have distinctive pale marks round the lower hindwings, which shine almost white in the sunshine on old specimens. But it is the underwings that are diagnostic: bright, variegated, with seven silver 'pearls' round the hindwing border, six or seven more within the wing, and the rest a contrasting mosaic of pale yellow and red-brown, outlined in black.

Young stages

The **egg** is laid, or dropped, singly among violets and nearby plants. It is rather tricky but by no means impossible to find; a tiny cone with 18–20 ridges down the sides, that is pale at first, turning grey as it develops.

Hibernation occurs in a curled leaf when the **caterpillar** is half grown. In spring it hides beneath vegetation, surfacing

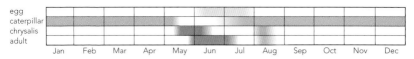

	Jan	Feb	Mar	Apr	May	Jun	Jul	Aug	Sep	Oct	Nov	Dec
egg												
caterpillar												
chrysalis												
adult												

briefly to nibble the lobes of violet leaves. When found it is unmistakable and very different to the Pearl-bordered Fritillary, due to 12 distinctive rows of amber cones that protude from the dark brown body.

The **chrysalis** is dark brown with silver points and is beautifully camouflaged among the vegetation in which it hangs.

Habitat and behaviour

This and the Pearl-bordered Fritillary share several habitats and fly together in some places in early June, despite the frightful declines experienced by both. Of the two, this is found in moister, grassier places where violets are abundant, and it is more tolerant of shading, although it too needs frequent clearings to survive. It is much scarcer on dry soils and, in the eastern half of England, is virtually confined to woods. Throughout the wetter west it also breeds in open habitats: search on sea cliffs, scrubby valley sides, moist hollows on moors and heaths and in rough sheltered grassland, especially near woodland edges. Common dog violet (*Viola riviniana*) is the main foodplant in the south, with marsh violet (*V. palustris*) important in the north.

Except on Welsh and northern moorlands, typical colonies are self-contained, breed in small discrete areas, and contain fewer than 200 adults, although huge numbers can briefly develop in large woodland clearings or on freshly burnt valley sides. In fine weather, the males flit and glide swiftly above the ground in a restless search for females, pausing only to gorge on nectar. The females are more secretive, but periodically emerge to flutter over violets, lay eggs and feed.

Distribution and status

This butterfly is absent from Ireland but is the most widespread and commonest of the small Fritillaries elsewhere. It is particularly well distributed on the Scottish mainland, where it is locally common in large areas of the west, but much scarcer in the extreme south-east and north-west (where emergence is later), and absent from the Caithness lowlands. Most large isles possess colonies, except for Islay, the Outer Hebrides, Orkneys and Shetlands. Elsewhere, colonies are locally common in the English Lake District and lowland Wales, and in Cornwall and Devon, especially on Dartmoor and along the scrubby coast. Huge declines have occurred everywhere else in England, and look set to continue. Apart from one or two sites in Yorkshire, Sussex, Hampshire and Dorset, it is now extinct in the eastern two-thirds of England, having once been widespread and plentiful. Shady woods, land drainage, agricultural improvements and the general tidying up of the countryside have all contributed to this decline.

confirmed range

129

PEARL-BORDERED FRITILLARY *Boloria euphrosyne*

Adult identification

Average wingspan 44 mm (♂) to 47 mm (♀)

The undersurface of the hindwing is the most distinctive feature of this small springtime Fritillary. The background is a mosaic of orange and yellow, with seven silver 'pearls' along the outer border and another two near the body, one each side of a central orange cell containing a black spot. The Small Pearl-bordered Fritillary

▲ *The seven silver 'pearls' that border the hindwing give this Fritillary its name.*

(page 40) has the same border, but at least six or seven silver patches towards the body and its background is richer brown, producing a more contrasting pattern. Marsh, Heath and Glanville Fritillaries (pages 40–41) have no silver patches and no central black spot.

The upperwings are bright orange with black veins, crossbars, and black spots towards the edges (page 40). They are almost identical to those of the Small Pearl-bordered Fritillary, so the under-wings should always be examined. Other small Fritillaries are less golden with thicker black veins, and none has black spots on the upper forewing.

Young stages

The **egg** is laid singly on or near violets, and not hard to find on good sites. Yellow at first, but darkening as the embryo develops, it is conical with 20–25 fine ridges running from top to bottom.

The **caterpillar** lives solitarily and hibernates among dead vegetation when small. It can sometimes be found in its last stage in April, basking openly on dead leaves or nibbling violet leaves.

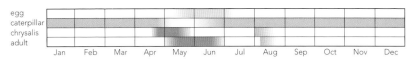

	Jan	Feb	Mar	Apr	May	Jun	Jul	Aug	Sep	Oct	Nov	Dec
egg												
caterpillar												
chrysalis												
adult												

Bright yellow bristles on a black body distinguish this from related caterpillars, although note that the bristles are black on some individuals.

The grey-brown **chrysalis** is usually too well hidden to find, suspended like a dead leaf among dense vegetation.

Habitat and behaviour

This was traditionally a woodland Fritillary, but today most colonies inhabit scrubby western hills where gorse or bracken is regularly burnt or cut back, while in Scotland many sites are woodland pasture, where grazing keeps the ground flora sparse and open. In the Burren (Ireland) and the English Lake District, it is found on sheltered limestone pavement. In all four situations, close-knit colonies breed in warm, sunny clearings where a flush of young violets has developed after the clearance of a shady plot. Common dog violet (*Viola riviniana*) and marsh violet (*V. palustris*) are the main foodplants in the south and north respectively. Typical colonies consist of a few tens of adults in a small clearing, but enormous populations can develop when an ancient wood is felled and replanted; these, alas, seldom last long before being shaded out. In the past, piecemeal coppicing created ideal conditions, allowing this not very mobile butterfly to follow the woodman round his wood, breeding each year in a new clearing.

The males of this Fritillary are delightful as they flit and glide across woodland clearings and rides, skimming above the ground flora and dipping towards bushes in their search for females. The latter fly less often, but are conspicuous when fluttering round violets or feeding on the nectar of bugle and other spring flowers.

Distribution and status

Until the 1950s this was a common butterfly in English and Welsh woods, at least on dry soils. Since then there has been an extraordinary decline. The main culprit is the virtual cessation of coppicing and the increased shadiness of deciduous and conifer woods. Today, it has virtually disappeared from England, apart from carefully conserved relic populations in Yorkshire, Sussex and the New Forest. Things are marginally better in Devon, where it occurs locally, sometimes in abundance, in sunny dry woodland and on some gorsy hills. Although much reduced in the Lake District, large populations breed on carefully managed reserves near Morecambe Bay.

In Ireland, it is restricted to the Burren, where it still plentiful and to be expected on sheltered limestone pavement where farmers regularly cut back the hazel scrub. The current British stronghold is the west and Highland areas of Scotland, where scattered colonies survive on the edges of deciduous wood pasture.

▓▓ confirmed
range

HIGH BROWN FRITILLARY *Argynnis adippe*

Adult identification

Average wingspan 60 mm (♂) to 67 mm (♀)

High Brown (HB) and Dark Green (DG) Fritillaries (pages 41–42) look very similar, with black spots on large golden upperwings and greenish-orange underwings that differ from the Silver-washed Fritillary (page 42) in possessing large clear-cut

▲ The High Brown Fritillary is best identified when it perches with its wings closed. Note the band of small silver dots within red haloes towards the outer edge of the hindwing.

silver spots, each outlined in black. HB and DG Fritillaries are distinguished by the following:

Upperwings
- Scent cells over the second and third vein up form elevated, glossy black streaks in the centre of the male HB's forewing. These are inconspicuous on male DGs and absent on females.
- Female DGs have paler spots round the outer edges.

Underwings
- The HB always has a row of small blurred red eyes with silver pupils on the hindwing, between the two outer bands of large silver spots. DGs do not.
- The DG has obvious silver spots down the outer edge of the forewing; the HB has none or, at most, two to three blurred patches in the corner.
- The background colour of the DG's hindwing is greener, but this varies.

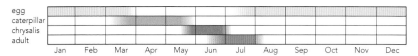

	Jan	Feb	Mar	Apr	May	Jun	Jul	Aug	Sep	Oct	Nov	Dec
egg												
caterpillar												
chrysalis												
adult												

Young stages

The **egg** is a pink cone, turning silver-grey during winter, with 13–15 ridges from the base upwards, most of which reach the top. It is laid singly on dead vegetation near violets and is hard to find (see Habitat).

The solitary **caterpillar** wanders freely between violets, often hiding beneath dead leaves. Fully grown, it has 12 rings of bristles and occurs in two colour forms: dark brown with a white stripe and pink bristles, or red-brown with a white stripe.

The **chrysalis** looks like a dead leaf and is completely hidden, suspended among vegetation. Its rather glossy body is dark brown with gold points.

Habitat and behaviour

The High Brown Fritillary breeds in sunny sheltered areas containing scattered shrubs and a warm sparse ground flora in which violets are abundant. Eggs are laid deep within a bush, young coppice stool or dry leaf litter beneath sparse bracken, and the caterpillar basks on the sunny edge or roams the open ground eating common dog violet (*Viola riviniana*). Periodic clearings, fire or grazing are essential to regenerate the extensive flushes of violets needed by this species.

Once, colonies were found in clearings in many of the large woods and forests of England and Wales, but almost all have disappeared during the past 70 years. The majority of modern woods are simply too shady for breeding, and new clearings too isolated from existing sites. In the west, surviving colonies breed in rough grassland and scrubby hillsides adjoining woodland, while in Cumbria they breed in sheltered scrubby areas of broken limestone; they often fly with the Dark Green Fritillary in both regions.

On all sites, the butterfly lives in fairly compact colonies, although emigrants may also be found some kilometres away. In both woodland and scrub, the adults fly more around the canopy than do smaller Fritillaries, roosting in the higher bushes at night and in bad weather. Flight is rapid and soaring, but they also feed avidly on bramble and thistle flowers, and can then be closely approached.

Distribution and status

The High Brown Fritillary was once locally common in large woods throughout Wales and much of England, especially on well-drained soils. Now it is one of our rarest and most rapidly declining species. Today it is confined to the Alun Valley, south Wales, to one valley on Exmoor, to the southern fringe of Dartmoor, and to the Morecambe Bay limestones, where it has shown a welcome increase due to targeted conservation management.

confirmed range

DARK GREEN FRITILLARY *Argynnis aglaja*

Adult identification

Average wingspan 63 mm (♂) to 69 mm (♀)

Dark Green and High Brown Fritillaries are often confused, due mainly to the popular yardstick that the former is restricted to rough grassland and the latter to woodland. This simply is not true; both fly together on some sites, but

▲ *The male of this mating pair of Dark Green Fritillaries has his wings half open, whilst the female shows the green and silver underwings that are a feature of this species.*

note that the High Brown Fritillary is now excessively rare. See pages 41–42 for features that distinguish these and also the Silver-washed Fritillary.

Note, on this species, paler spots round the edges of the female's upper-wings; no noticeable scent marks on the more golden males; greenish under hind-wings (especially in females) that have no red eyes with silver pupils between the outer rows of silver spots; the presence of silver spots on the under forewing.

The above features are constant, but adults vary in other respects through their range. Irish upperwings are redder-brown; in north-west Scotland and many Western Isles, adults are larger (except on Orkney), much darker and have greener under-wings with very large silver patches.

Young stages

The **egg** is conical with 19–22 ridges from the bottom which do not all reach the top. Yellow at first, it develops purple

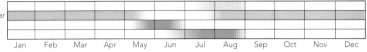

	Jan	Feb	Mar	Apr	May	Jun	Jul	Aug	Sep	Oct	Nov	Dec
egg												
caterpillar												
chrysalis												
adult												

bands and is hard to find on or near bushy clumps of violets.

The **caterpillar** can sometimes be found basking, moving across the ground, or feeding in sunshine on the lobes, tips and edges of violet leaves, leaving large bite marks. When fully grown, the body has a glossy sheen of purple-black, with white speckles, red spots along the side, and black bristles.

The **chrysalis** has a dark brown abdomen, black wing cases, head and thorax, and is completely hidden in a tussock or dense vegetation.

Habitat and behaviour

This spectacular butterfly is generally found in more exposed places than our other Fritillaries, but note that low numbers sometimes occur in woodland rides and that, nowadays, one is very much more likely to see this than the High Brown Fritillary in British woods. However, wild open sites are more typical habitat, especially coastal cliffs, undercliffs, dunes, moorland, flowery downs and unfertilized rough grassland. Depending on the habitat, caterpillars eat various violets including hairy (*Viola hirta*), marsh (*V. palustris*) and common dog (*V. riviniana*). Eggs are laid among large isolated bushy clumps of violet or in spots where smaller plants dominate. On most sites, the sward is around 5–15 cm tall, kept open by erosion, periodic burning or light grazing.

Adult Dark Green Fritillaries are fast and powerful fliers. They soar up and down hillsides and are approachable only when pausing to feed on thistles and other flowers. Despite their powers of flight, adults stay within fairly discrete colonies. Some consist of vast numbers, but the butterfly is more often seen in ones or twos.

Distribution and status

Although countless lowland populations have been destroyed by agricultural improvements, this remains our most widely distributed and, in many areas, commonest Fritillary. Its stronghold is the coastline of Ireland, Scotland, Wales and England, except in the east where it is very scarce. With that exception, it is still to be expected, though seldom in numbers, in all wild coastal habitats around Britain. It is equally well distributed on most islands as far north as Orkney; many beautiful and distinctive races have developed on these isolated sites. Inland, it is much more local, although well distributed throughout the Highlands and in other rough hilly areas of Scotland, Wales and south-west England. It is much scarcer in the rest of England, having been eliminated from most flat landscapes. Nevertheless, fine populations survive on some unfertilized hills, especially in the Cotswolds, Salisbury Plain and other southern chalk downs.

▓▓▓ confirmed range

135

SILVER-WASHED FRITILLARY *Argynnis paphia*

Adult identification

Average wingspan 72 mm (♂) to 76 mm (♀)

This is the largest, most magnificent and the latest of our Fritillaries to emerge. The male's upperwings are unmistakable; note the deep orange background, large

▲ *A male Silver-washed Fritillary (below) and the darker female basking in a Surrey wood.*

black spots and lines, and four broad streaks of black scent cells along the central veins of the forewing. The female lacks these streaks, but has larger spots on a duller background, thus creating an impression of a much browner colour both at rest and in flight; no other large Fritillary is so dark. It is the under hindwing (page 42) that is most distinctive in both sexes: there are four wishy-washy silver streaks down a greenish background, very different from the discrete silver patches of other large Fritillaries.

Some females have a dusky green ground colour on the upperwings and pink on the under forewing (page 42). This beautiful form, called *valezina*, is unmistakable when settled or in flight.

Young stages

Each **egg** is laid singly usually 1–1.5 m up a tree trunk that has violets underneath. It is pale, conical with about 25 vertical ridges, and quite easy to find in late July

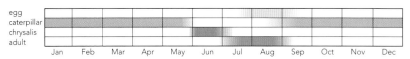

	Jan	Feb	Mar	Apr	May	Jun	Jul	Aug	Sep	Oct	Nov	Dec
egg												
caterpillar												
chrysalis												
adult												

among chinks in bark on the mossy side of a suitable tree.

The **caterpillar** hibernates before descending to feed in spring. When fully grown the body is velvety brown, with darker streaks, twin yellow stripes down the back, and numerous long bristly spines of which two point forwards over the head, like horns. Look for it in May and early June, basking on dead leaves or eating the lobes of violet leaves in sunny pockets within woods.

The **chrysalis** is beautiful but unlikely to be found since it is camouflaged to look like a dead leaf hanging, wet with dew, among dense vegetation.

Habitat and behaviour

This grand Fritillary lives principally in woodland, but also flies and breeds along nearby hedgebanks and lanes in sheltered valleys in Ireland and the west. Slightly darker woods are preferred to those inhabited by other Fritillaries, although colonies are soon shaded out of dense conifer plantations. The best sites are large, recently thinned broadleaved woods, where numerous shafts of light penetrate to the forest floor. The female flutters across the half-lit ground and, on touching violets, flies up to lay on the nearest tree. Common dog violet (*Viola riviniana*) is the main food of the caterpillar.

Silver-washed Fritillaries live in fairly compact colonies, but also stray into neighbouring copses and spinneys that do not support permanent populations. It is a powerful yet elegant flier, preferring sunny glades, rides and edges when not egg-laying. Both sexes roost high among tree branches, but swoop down in sunshine to feed on bramble and other flowers or soar up to the canopy to drink aphid honeydew. Courtship is spectacular; the female flies rapidly in a straight line along a woodland ride with the male in hot pursuit looping around her.

Distribution and status

Despite many extinctions, it has fared much better than other woodland Fritillaries, perhaps because it can survive in slightly shadier woods. Colonies are commonest in the west, and probably breed in all woods and along many lanes throughout Devon, Somerset, east Cornwall, south Wales and Ireland. It may be locally abundant in all these regions after a hot summer. It also inhabits most woods in Herefordshire, Somerset, Gloucestershire, south Wiltshire, Dorset, Hampshire and the Weald of Surrey and Sussex. However, it is much more localized in the West Midlands and has disappeared – or virtually gone – from the East Midlands, Kent and East Anglia.

Valezina females are found regularly over a broad area of the central south and may constitute ten percent of females in a warm summer.

confirmed range

valezina normal range; very rare north

137

Adult identification

Average wingspan 42 mm (♂) to 48 mm (♀); very variable

Although highly variable in both size and colour, this has, in general, duller, less distinct, and certainly less golden markings than Britain's other Fritillaries. The upperwings are reddish-orange, with yellow or white patches, and black veins

▲ *A male Marsh Fritillary perches on dead vegetation on an overgrown bog.*

and crossbars that may be blurred. It is the only Fritillary to have one row of black dots around the bottom edge on both sides of the hindwings but none on either side of the forewing, not even on the tip of the underside (see Glanville Fritillary page 140, and Duke of Burgundy page 110). Like the rare Glanville and Heath Fritillaries, the underwings have no trace of silver; the general impression is of dull black and orange on a dull yellow background.

Young stages

Females lay prodigious batches of glossy yellow **eggs**, heaped up like hard fish roe on a devil's bit scabious leaf. Each is oval with about 20 narrow ridges from the top to halfway down. Egg clusters soon turn red and can sometimes be found, but the **caterpillars** are easy to spot. They are bristly and uniformly black except for tiny white freckles on the sides, and bask openly in weak sunlight. In summer they live gregariously on a web spun over the foodplant before hibernating in a denser nest of silk among taller vegetation. In spring, caterpillars split into small groups

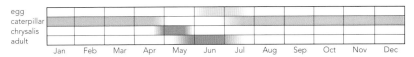

	Jan	Feb	Mar	Apr	May	Jun	Jul	Aug	Sep	Oct	Nov	Dec
egg												
caterpillar												
chrysalis												
adult												

as they grow larger and eventually live singly, but are still conspicuous.

The **chrysalis** is formed among dense vegetation and is hard to find. It is cream with black marks and orange points.

Habitat and behaviour

The Marsh Fritillary is found in flowery open grassland where devil's bit scabious (*Succisa pratensis*) is abundant. Breeding is mainly on medium-sized plants with leaves around 5–15 cm tall, whereas small growths in short turf and large plants in dense vegetation are both avoided. It lives in two very different types of habitat – damp unimproved meadows and boggy hollows where there is occasional or light grazing, or dry chalk and limestone downland that is lightly cropped or recently abandoned.

The butterfly lives in compact colonies but occasionally strays in warm years. Numbers fluctuate greatly on any site from a few tens to many thousands of adults, depending on the food supply, weather, and the proportion of caterpillars that were killed by parasitic wasps. Spectacular outbreaks occurred regularly in the past, but are unknown nowadays, when vast swarms of caterpillars blackened acres of meadowland, eating out the scabiouses before dying in countless numbers through starvation.

Female Marsh Fritillaries usually perch half hidden among tussocks, and may be so laden with eggs that flight is possible only in the warmest weather. The males are more active, and have a curious flitting flight, skimming low over the vegetation as they scan for females.

Distribution and status

This beautiful Fritillary is one of our (and Europe's) most rapidly declining species. Most former wetland sites have been destroyed by drainage and agricultural improvements, and – apart from an introduction to Lincolnshire – it is now extinct in the entire eastern half of its former English and Scottish range. In Wiltshire and Dorset it is close to extinction on boggy farmland, but has actually spread on chalk and limestone downs, and although still extremely local, the military ranges of Salisbury Plain are today one of its UK strongholds. Others include the surviving Culm grasslands of Cornwall and north Devon, the Rhos pastures and heathy commons of south Wales, and central west Scotland, especially the Isle of Islay. The bogs and meadows of Ireland remain a major international stronghold, but it has now become much more localized there due to reclamation and drainage. Nevertheless, recent surveys show that the Marsh Fritillary is still widely distributed and under-recorded in Ireland, where it is now the focus of a major conservation initiative.

confirmed range

GLANVILLE FRITILLARY *Melitaea cinxia*

Adult identification

Average wingspan 41 mm (♂) to 47 mm (♀)

Both sexes look similar and, like all Fritillaries (pages 40–42), the upperwings have a chequered pattern of black and orange-brown. The dark lines are heavy

communal
caterpillars

▲ *A freshly emerged Glanville Fritillary perching on thrift on the southern coast of the Isle of Wight.*

on this species, and there is a row of black spots in orange circles along the bottom edge of the hindwing. The under hindwing is bright and distinctive, with two bands of orange marks, each outlined in black, on a cream and white background, and more spots near the outer edge. There are also spots on the tip of the under forewing.

The Marsh Fritillary (page 138) has a similar pattern but no spots on the under forewing, and it is duller with more orange on the under hindwings. Moreover, the Glanville Fritillary is confined to the Isle of Wight, where, of the smaller Fritillaries, only the Pearl-bordered and Small Pearl-bordered (just) survive. These have silver on the underwings and the upper forewings are more golden with black spots.

Young stages

The **eggs** are laid in batches of 50–200 on ribwort plantains (see Habitat). Each is

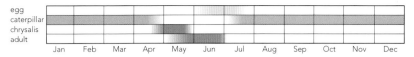

	Jan	Feb	Mar	Apr	May	Jun	Jul	Aug	Sep	Oct	Nov	Dec
egg												
caterpillar												
chrysalis												
adult												

yellow and oval, with around 20 ridges from the top to about halfway down.

The **caterpillars** are extremely conspicuous at all stages. They live gregariously and have black spiny bodies with (when older) shining russet heads that distinguish them from other Fritillaries. When young they bask in hundreds on silk webs spun over plantains and eat the leaves. In September, an even more conspicuous dense hibernation nest is spun among tall grass, often away from their foodplant. The following spring they grow large and spread out in black swarms over the plantains. Fully grown caterpillars scatter to pupate singly in dense grass and crevices.

The **chrysalis** is purple-grey with black and orange spots, but very difficult to find.

Habitat and behaviour

This is essentially a central European Fritillary that can just survive in the warmest spots of Britain. It is confined to the south coasts of southern islands, breeding in pockets among crumbling cliffs and undercliffs, and in sheltered south-facing valleys. Search where the terrain is unstable, allowing thousands of ribwort plantains (*Plantago lanceolata*) to develop among a sparse sward. The caterpillars eat vast quantities of the young plantain then, rather than starve, switch to old growths or to buckshorn plantain. Colonies wax and wane rapidly according to the food supply which is dependent on annual slippage and falls along unstable cliffs, for plantains soon decline where a dense sward develops.

The adults live in more or less compact colonies, although females also stray to lay eggs along cliff tops. Glanville Fritillaries are conspicuous butterflies with a deceptively fast flight of whirring wingbeats punctuated by graceful glides. The males patrol low spots and nooks, sometimes in hundreds, and both sexes can be closely approached when feeding on the nectar from thrift, trefoil and other flowers.

Distribution and status

The Glanville Fritillary is one of our rarest butterflies, although it may be numerous where it does occur. Colonies breed around the coasts of most of the Channel Isles and in pockets along much of the southern coastline of the Isle of Wight, especially on sandstone exposures in the western half. There are about 12 more or less permanent colonies on the island, some containing several hundred adults in good years. From these, strays leave to lay anywhere along the cliff edges and paths, as well as in more conventional habitats.

Odd nests are occasionally found on the chalk downs of the Isle of Wight, and English entomologists often release adults on the mainland. These sometimes establish temporary colonies: two current examples exist, in south Hampshire and on a limestone promontory in Somerset, where it has persisted for 30 years.

■■■ confirmed range

141

HEATH FRITILLARY *Melitaea athalia*

Adult identification

Average wingspan 40 mm (♂) to 44 mm (♀)

The males of this rare Fritillary are slightly darker and smaller than the females, but otherwise the sexes look similar. The upperwings have the usual Fritillary pattern – a network of dark lines and bars on an orange-brown back-

communal caterpillars

▲ *A male of the rare Heath Fritillary basking on oak leaves on one of its last surviving British sites.*

ground – but this is the only species with no brown spots around the edges (pages 40–42). The same absence of both spots and silver patches distinguishes the underwings. These have an elegant pattern of fine veins and orange marks against a cream and white background on the hindwing, whilst the forewing, although usually hidden, is dull orange with a few dark stripes.

Young stages

The **eggs** are laid in large clusters of 50–150, usually under a tough bramble or dead leaf near one of the caterpillar's foodplants (see Habitat). Each is small (0.6 mm tall), conical with about 26 vertical ridges, and is pale yellow at first turning grey as the caterpillar develops. Egg batches are well hidden, but the young **caterpillars** can be found on good sites, in groups of 10–20 on silk spun over their foodplants. They hibernate in similar groups among dead leaves, but live more freely the following spring and bask openly on dead leaves.

	Jan	Feb	Mar	Apr	May	Jun	Jul	Aug	Sep	Oct	Nov	Dec
egg												
caterpillar												
chrysalis												
adult												

Fully grown caterpillars are easy to find in May, especially on sites with sparse vegetation. They have black heads and bodies, with parallel rows of bristly white and amber cones down their backs.

The **chrysalis** is very pretty but, alas, too well hidden among dead leaves to find. It is white with numerous brown and black markings.

Habitat and behaviour

The Heath Fritillary lives in discrete colonies in exceptionally warm and sunny habitats, sheltered by shrubs or trees, where the caterpillar's foodplants grow in abundance among an otherwise sparse ground flora on poor, well-drained or stony soils. Depending on the site, the main plants eaten are cow-wheat (*Melampyrum pratense*), ribwort plantain (*Plantago lanceolata*), and germander speedwell (*Veronica chamaedrys*), although other plants, including foxglove (*Digitalis purpurea*), may be tackled by older caterpillars.

Typical sites are freshly cut woodland (cow-wheat), recently afforested old grassland (plantain), and heaths on valley sides on Exmoor (cow-wheat again). The habitat is usually ephemeral; the butterfly colonizes a clearing, increases at best to thousands of adults after two to four years, then may be entirely shaded out three to seven years later. Unfortunately, colonies are unable to move far, and the lack of a continuous supply of new habitats near to existing sites, as formerly occurred when woods were coppiced, has resulted in numerous extinctions.

Where it survives, the Heath Fritillary is a conspicuous butterfly. Males incessantly patrol woodland rides and clearings, occasionally in hundreds, with a weak gliding flight, pausing only to feed. The females are more secretive, but are also conspicuous on flowers.

Distribution and status

The Heath Fritillary has always been scarce and confined to southern England, but has suffered numerous local extinctions in recent decades and is now one of our rarest butterflies. Fortunately, it was saved from the brink of extinction, and today most remaining sites are either nature reserves or actively managed to maintain suitable conditions, albeit with mixed results. At present, about 23 colonies – some very large – survive on reserves in its old stronghold, the Blean Forest woods near Canterbury in Kent. Its other recent stronghold, certain Exmoor hillsides, has also seen a welcome recovery thanks to improved management since the turn of the century. Elsewhere, reintroduced populations in west Devon and in four south-east Essex woods continue to thrive, but these are balanced by further extinctions in east Cornwall.

▨▨▨ confirmed range

SPECKLED WOOD *Pararge aegeria*

Adult identification

Average wingspan 47 mm (♂) to 50 mm (♀)

This medium-sized Brown often basks with its wings open, revealing an unmistakable pattern of creamy-yellow patches on a deep chocolate background. There

▲ *This spectacular and unmistakable male Speckled Wood is fond of basking on warm dead leaves, where it is well camouflaged.*

are three separate black eyes with white pupils in the patches towards the edge of each hindwing and another eye near the top corner of each forewing. The males have slightly smaller and more blurred yellow markings than the females, and in both sexes the patches are a little paler in the summer brood.

The underwings (page 43) are beautifully patterned in grey and brown, and resemble a dead leaf when the wings are closed. There are faint marks like mould-spots on the lower wing and a conspicuous eyespot at the top corner of the forewing. Note its habit of flying in shady places, where its chequered wings perfectly match the dappled light. No other butterfly is likely to be confused with this species.

In warmer climates on the continent, a more orange variety of Speckled Wood exists that looks superficially like the Wall Brown (page 146).

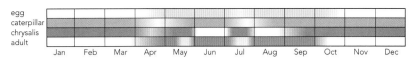

	Jan	Feb	Mar	Apr	May	Jun	Jul	Aug	Sep	Oct	Nov	Dec
egg												
caterpillar												
chrysalis												
adult												

Young stages

The **egg** is globular with fine striations on the surface and pale yellow with a glassy sheen. Laid singly on grass blades half-shaded beneath shrubs, it is rather difficult to find.

The **caterpillar** is also quite elusive, although it feeds by day on sheltered grasses. It is pale green with faint white and yellow lines, and the 'tails' are white with grey hairs.

The **chrysalis** hangs beneath dense vegetation and is virtually impossible to find. It varies in colour from pale green to dark and even brownish-green. The Speckled Wood can hibernate as either caterpillar or chrysalis, thus leading to a complicated sequence of adult broods and emergence dates.

Habitat and behaviour

The Speckled Wood lives in shadier places than any other native butterfly apart from the White Admiral. Eggs are laid on tender blades of grass growing sparsely in weak light on the woodland floor, or, in more open situations, beneath shrubs. Cocksfoot (*Dactylis glomerata*) and couch (*Agropyron repens*) are pre-ferred, but false brome and Yorkshire fog are also used. Typical sites are dimly lit broad-leaved woods, abandoned cop-pices, and conifer plantations, although it is shaded out of the latter once the crop matures beyond middle age. The Speckled Wood may also be seen flutter-ing in dappled light along leafy lanes, tall shady hedgerows (including mature gardens) and among scrub, especially on heavy soils and in damp spots.

The adults feed mainly out of sight, drinking honeydew on treetops, but may descend to jostle with Meadow Browns, Ringlets and Skippers on bramble blos-som in sunny woodland rides. They are usually seen in ones or twos, especially the male which occupies a beam of light in which he perches, basks, and indulges in dancing fluttery flights. He leaves only to ward off other males or to chase females, then returns to his original sunbeam where he can be closely observed for long periods.

Distribution and status

The Speckled Wood became scarce in the 19th century, but has increased its numbers and range greatly during the past 75 years, no doubt encouraged by the shadier con-ditions that have been developing in most British woods, and by the warming climate. Today, it is a common butterfly in almost all woods and copses throughout Ireland, Wales and England south of a line from Cumbria to southern Yorkshire. As in the south, it is spreading rapidly from its two isolated strongholds in northern Scotland, which have now more-or-less joined to form a solid band of colonies stretching from some Western Isles to the Moray Firth.

▓▓▓ confirmed
range

WALL BROWN *Lasiommata megera*

Adult identification

Average wingspan 44 mm (♂) to 46 mm (♀)

The Wall Brown (or Wall) is usually seen basking with open wings, revealing bright orange uppersides with dark borders, veins and wavy crosslines, and dusky areas near the body. Both sexes have a conspicuous white-pupilled black eye-

▲ *The Wall Brown usually basks on rocks or bare ground in rough open grassland.*

spot in the top corner of each forewing, and a row of four smaller eyespots around the lower edge of each hindwing.

The underside of the forewing is a paler version of the upperside, but the under hindwing is different (page 43), being pearl grey with brown zigzag lines and a row of six eyespots towards the outer edge, each composed of a white-pupilled black spot surrounded by rings of yellow and brown. The bottom spot often has a double pupil. With its wings closed, the Wall blends beautifully with the bare ground on which it habitually sits. In flight, it looks so golden as to be confused with a Comma or a Fritillary, but at rest the eyespots and pattern are unmistakable.

Young stages

The **egg** is smooth, almost spherical, and green soon turning to glassy white. It is quite easy to find, singly or in small clusters, on grass roots or fine blades dangling into little sunspots in warm bare recesses and overhangs.

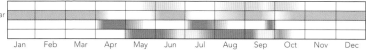

	Jan	Feb	Mar	Apr	May	Jun	Jul	Aug	Sep	Oct	Nov	Dec
egg												
caterpillar												
chrysalis												
adult												

The **caterpillar** feeds at night on grasses in warm pockets or among bare ground, but is quite difficult to find. It is bluish green when fully grown, with faint white stripes.

The **chrysalis** hangs inconspicuously among grass clumps and is unlikely to be found. It varies from pale to very dark green and even black, with white or yellow spots.

Habitat and behaviour

Unlike its closest relative, the Speckled Wood, this golden Brown lives in rough open grassland sites where there is plenty of sunbaked ground. The caterpillar feeds on several native coarse grasses, including tor (*Brachypodium pinnatum*), wood false brome (*B. sylvaticum*), cocksfoot (*Dactylis glomerata*), Yorkshire fog (*Holcus lanatus*) and wavy-hair grass (*Deschampsia flexuosa*). Dense swards are ignored, egg-laying being confined to occasional plants growing on the edges of bare sunspots, such as hoofprints, rabbit scrapes, among rocks, and the crumbling edges of paths. Typical sites are thin-soiled hedgebanks, old quarries, wasteland and disturbed ground, eroding cliffs, and unfertilized downs that are criss-crossed by paths and sheepwalk. It may also be found along road verges and field edges, and in woods, where egg-laying occurs on grass growing sparsely under the sunny sides of shrubs.

Walls live in small discrete colonies. There are normally two adult broods, with the second emergence more numerous than the spring one. After warm summers, there may be a small third brood lasting well into autumn. The adults perch in bare patches of ground, often on paths, basking with their wings two-thirds open. When disturbed they fly rapidly for a few metres, then settle farther on in another bare patch. The males also patrol areas in search of mates around midday, but switch to perching behaviour in the morning and late afternoon.

Distribution and status

The Wall Brown was once a common butterfly of rough ground and unfertilized grassland in most of England and Wales, except in the mountains. However, it has experienced major fluctuations over the centuries, and since the 1970s became scarce or disappeared in large areas of the Midlands and central southern England. Yet at the same time it expanded northwards along the coast and inland in Yorkshire, Durham, Lancashire and Northumberland, and far along the coast of south-west Scotland. At present, it is commonest near the coastline of England and Wales, including the Isle of Man. It is also widely, but rather sparsely distributed on the drier soils of central and southern Ireland, but again it is much commoner along the coast.

confirmed range

MOUNTAIN RINGLET *Erebia epiphron*

Adult identification

Average wingspan 35 mm (♂) to 38 mm (♀)

This, our second smallest Brown, has slender wings that are deep velvet-brown on the uppersides and very hairy near the body, as indeed is the body

▲ *In fine weather, the male Mountain Ringlet basks for long periods on tussocks of grass. When the weather is dull it sits deep among mat grass and is very difficult to spot.*

itself. Towards the outer edge of each wing is a band of orange blotches, each containing a black dot with no white pupil except, occasionally, on females. Typically, there are four dots on each forewing and three on each hindwing, but this is very variable, as is the sharpness of the blotches. Males tend to be smaller than females and have more blurred markings, but otherwise the sexes look similar. The underwings resemble the upperwings, with less or even no orange blotches and fainter dots (page 45).

Only the Scotch Argus is at all similar (page 150), but it is considerably larger than the Mountain Ringlet, with sharper markings and conspicuous black eye-spots containing gleaming white pupils. Note, too, the restricted range, earlier emergence date, and higher altitude of the Mountain Ringlet.

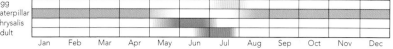

	Jan	Feb	Mar	Apr	May	Jun	Jul	Aug	Sep	Oct	Nov	Dec
egg												
caterpillar												
chrysalis												
adult												

On the continent there are many similar species of *Erebia*, most of which also live on mountainsides.

Young stages

The **egg** is barrel-shaped and quite tall (1 mm), with 18–20 ridges running from top to bottom. It is pale yellow with orange blotches, and is laid at the bottom of tussocks of mat grass.

The **caterpillar** hibernates when quite small deep in its tussock, and resumes feeding the following spring. When full grown it is green with conspicuous white stripes and twin buff-coloured tails. It climbs mat grass at night to feed on the tender leaftips. Pupation occurs low down among vegetation.

The **chrysalis** is very pretty: pale green with many neat brown stripes.

Habitat and behaviour

The Mountain Ringlet lives in discrete grassy areas high up on open mountain sides in the Lake District and the Highlands of Scotland. The caterpillars feed on mat grass (*Nardus stricta*) but the range of this butterfly is much more restricted than that of its foodplant. Colonies are found at altitudes of 200–1,000 m, but usually at 500–800 m, on damp *Nardus* grassland that is quite tall, yet lightly cropped by sheep or deer. Search for colonies especially along gullies running down the mountain side and in swampy hollows bordering streams.

This butterfly flies strictly within self-contained colonies, which may contain several thousand adults on the best sites. In dull weather they sit deep among the mat grass and are easily overlooked. They suddenly emerge in sunshine, basking in vast numbers with their wings wide open, or fluttering very slowly above the matted vegetation.

Distribution and status

The Mountain Ringlet has a highly restricted range in Britain, but where it does occur it is locally common, especially in Scotland. It is maintaining its status well, despite some losses at lower altitudes due, no doubt, to the warmer climate.

There are two main centres – at high altitudes in the central English Lake District and in Scotland, where adults tend to be larger. In Scotland, it lives in the Grampians, from Glen Clova eastwards to Ben Vain and Ben Nevis, and as far north as the hills south of Newtonmore, Inverness. There is also a colony on Ben Lomond. Due to the difficulty of its terrain, the Mountain Ringlet is likely to have been under-recorded in its main Scottish range. There are also unsubstantiated reports from north and south-west Scotland, which are largely discounted by local experts. Irish records (not mapped) date from the 19th century, and their validity has been hotly disputed ever since.

■ confirmed range

SCOTCH ARGUS *Erebia aethiops*

Adult identification

Average wingspan 35 mm (♂) to 40 mm (♀), smaller in north-east Scotland

The Scotch Argus has deep velvet-brown upperwings, enlivened by rust-coloured spots which are more or less separate on the hindwings but which merge into a bright band across each

▲ The Scotch Argus is virtually confined to Scotland in mountainous regions up to 500 m. The male, shown here, is smaller and darker than the female.

forewing. Conspicuous white-pupilled black eyespots are set amid the orange, typically three to each forewing and four to each hindwing.

At rest, the forewings are often tucked down, leaving just the under hindwings showing. These are brown with a blurred silver band, very like a dead leaf. The forewing, when protruded, is more conspicuous, with an orange band, a double eyespot near the outer tip, and a single eyespot farther down. Note that the Gatekeeper (page 156) has just a single black eye containing two white pupils on its under forewing and does not overlap in range.

Male Scotch Argus are smaller, darker and have redder bands than the females, and in north-east Scotland both sexes have smaller narrower wings. In south-west Scotland there is often a small fourth eye on the forewing. Only the smaller, rarer and duller Mountain Ringlet (page 148) is at all similar in Britain.

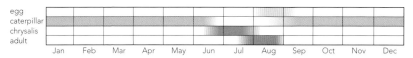

	Jan	Feb	Mar	Apr	May	Jun	Jul	Aug	Sep	Oct	Nov	Dec
egg												
caterpillar												
chrysalis												
adult												

Young stages

The **egg** is barrel-shaped with about 25 ridges running from top to bottom. It is straw-coloured with pink freckles and large, at least 1.3 mm tall. It is laid deep in tussocks of blue or purple moor grasses, and although hard to find in the wild is easily obtained from captive females.

The **caterpillar** hibernates when quite small and is fully grown by late June. It is then pale grey-green with green stripes, very like the Gatekeeper caterpillar except that the latter has uniformly white hairs whilst those on the Scotch Argus have brown tips. Look for it at dusk by searching the tender leaftips of moor grasses.

The **chrysalis** is pale brown and formed just below the ground in cells of moss in damp places.

Habitat and behaviour

The Scotch Argus inhabits rough boggy grassland in Scotland and the Lake District, where the caterpillars feed on purple moor grass (*Molinea caerulea*) and other grasses in Scotland, and on blue grass (*Sesleria caerulea*) in England. Colonies occur in mountainous regions up to 500 m altitude, in spots where the food grasses grow quite tall and dense. Typical sites are warm moist valleys and rough hillsides, especially along the south and eastern edges of woods or scrub. Smaller colonies may be found inside woods and young plantations, along rides, and in glades and recent clearings; a few inhabit sheltered open moorland.

This butterfly lives in discrete colonies containing over ten thousand adults on the best sites. Both sexes hide among rank grass in poor weather, but in sunshine they suddenly appear to feed on flowers, while the males search for mates, flying slowly at grasshead height between the tussocks, dipping down to investigate any brown leaflike object.

Distribution and status

The Scotch Argus is a northern species that was once found in several areas of Cumbria, West Yorkshire, Northumberland and the Durham coast. Today just two large English colonies survive, both on limestone grassland in the Lake District.

In Scotland there have been declines in the south-east, but the larger *caledonia* race remains locally common over large areas of the south-west, at low altitudes throughout the Highlands, and on many isles of the Inner Hebrides and the west coast, including Arran. The small dark *aethiops* race is also locally common in suitable habitats from east Ross-shire to north-east Perthshire. There is no evidence of a decline in recent decades; indeed new surveys found many overlooked colonies, especially in north Scotland.

▓▓▓ confirmed
range

MARBLED WHITE *Melanargia galathea*

Adult identification

Average wingspan 53 mm (♂) to 58 mm (♀)

This lovely medium-sized butterfly has a clear-cut pattern of black and white chequered markings on its wings, very different from our other native Browns, and unlikely to be confused with White butter-

▲ This marvellous chequerboard of a butterfly is quite different to any other Brown or White. The distinctive pattern is obvious even in flight as the Marbled White flaps its wings very slowly.

flies, since they do not have anything like so much black on them. Another difference from the Whites is a series of blue-centred black eyespots which are conspicuous, at rest, towards the outer edges of the under-wings. The Marbled White's chequered pattern is also recognizable during flight, partly because the wings are flapped very slowly. The ground colour on the under-wings varies somewhat from white to pale yellow, and the markings are less distinct, being grey on males and a dusky olive-green on the females (page 16).

Young stages

The **eggs** are dropped singly to the ground above patches of tall grass, and are impossible to find in the wild although easily obtained from captive females. They are white and almost spherical, with a slightly granulated surface.

The young **caterpillar** almost immed-iately hibernates. When fully grown the fol-

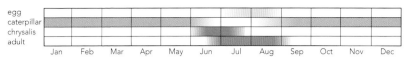

	Jan	Feb	Mar	Apr	May	Jun	Jul	Aug	Sep	Oct	Nov	Dec
egg												
caterpillar												
chrysalis												
adult												

lowing June it varies in colour from yellow-green to pale brown, with darker green lines down both forms and pink 'tails'. It hides by day at the base of grass clumps but ascends to eat blades at night, and can be found quite easily by torchlight.

The **chrysalis** is hidden in the soil beneath vegetation. It is an anaemic pale brown, and difficult to find.

Habitat and behaviour

The Marbled White lives in tall, but seldom dense, unfertilized grassland, in colonies with distinct boundaries: it may breed for years in one field and yet be absent from neighbouring land. This might be due to the species of native grass that are present. Red fescue (*Festuca rubra*) is perhaps essential in the caterpillar's diet, although sheep's fescue (*F. ovina*), timothy (*Phleum pratense*), cocksfoot (*Dactylis glomerata*) and tor grass (*Brachypodium pinnatum*) are also eaten. It may also need grass that is infected by fungi, whose poisons are deposited in the adult's conspicuous wings, thus deterring birds.

Colonies breed on a wide range of soils, including heavy clays, but are commonest on chalk and limestone. Look for it anywhere within its restricted range where wild grasses grow quite tall, and expect to find it on unfertilized open downland, cliffs and undercliffs. Other typical sites are woodland rides, road verges and embankments.

Many colonies contain a few tens of adults, but on lightly grazed or abandoned downs, thousands may be seen flapping lazily above the grassheads. They alight frequently to feed on knapweeds, scabious and other tall flowers, basking with the wings held open when the light is weak, for example in late afternoon. In the heat of the day they sit with their wings tightly closed, reflecting rather than absorbing the sun's rays.

Distribution and status

The Marbled White has a curiously restricted range, although in recent years it has spread to fill many gaps in east England. Expanding groups of colonies live in the Yorkshire Wolds and near Durham, several resulting from introductions, which may also explain its reappearance on many East Midlands sites. A further group of colonies lives near the south Wales coast. Colonies are common in unfertilized fields on the North Downs in Kent but still scarce, though spreading, in Surrey. In Sussex it is restricted to the South Downs. Only slightly farther west the Marbled White is a common and ubiquitous butterfly of unfertilized grasslands and woodland rides on suitable soils throughout central southern and south-west England, except for southwest Cornwall. Despite widespread losses within its main range due to agricultural improvements, this remains a common butterfly in southern regions that is expanding into new areas.

▓▓ confirmed
range

153

Adult identification

Average wingspan 55 mm (♂) to 60 mm (♀); about 32 mm closed

This, our largest Brown, can be confused with no other species. The sexes look similar although the female is slightly paler and larger. They always settle with the wings closed, with usually the forewings tucked out of sight so that only the under-

▲ *This Grayling has just alighted on a typical resting spot among bare chalk. Soon the forewing, with its conspicuous spot, will be hidden, making the butterfly hard to see. See also page 18.*

surfaces of the hindwings are visible. These are marbled in pale brown and dark and light grey, with no clear pattern although a zigzag boundary halfway in separates darker markings near the body from a paler outer half. All in all, it looks like grey bark or dirty sand, and is perfectly camouflaged against the bare spots of ground on which it settles. When the under forewings protrude they reveal a grey border and a brighter, almost orange centre containing two conspicuous black eyespots with white pupils. The upperwings are light brown with bright straw-coloured bands and distinctive eyespots, giving the Grayling a richer brighter appearance in flight than the underwings would suggest, although the overall impression is still of grey.

Young stages

The **egg** is laid singly on fine grasses, and is easily found on good sites. Search where its food grasses sprout in small tufts among sand or bare soil in warm sunny hoof-marks, path-edges or other perturbed spots. It is

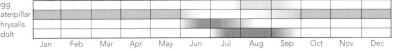

	Jan	Feb	Mar	Apr	May	Jun	Jul	Aug	Sep	Oct	Nov	Dec
egg												
caterpillar												
chrysalis												
adult												

gleaming white, almost spherical, and has 28 ridges running from top to bottom.

The **caterpillar** feeds at night on grass blades and rests deep in its tuft by day. Search by torchlight on evenings in early June; it is off-white with a greenish-brown head and clear yellow, brown and white stripes down its length. It pupates in a small earth cell about 5 mm under the ground.

The **chrysalis** is reddish-brown, buried, and impossible to find in the wild.

Habitat and behaviour

The Grayling inhabits unfertilized grasslands on a wide range of well-drained soils, including acid sandstones, shales and chalk hills. It is confined to the most arid places in Britain, where wild grasses grow sparsely among sand, rock or bare earth. Typical sites are well-grazed downs where chalk or limestone rubble shows through the turf, abandoned quarries, crumbling south-facing sea cliffs, and, especially, sand-dune systems and southern lowland heaths. It is the characteristic Brown of these two latter habitats. The caterpillars eat a range of grasses depending on geology, including bristle bent (*Agrostis setacea*), sheep's and red fescue (*Festuca ovina, F. rubra*), early hair-grass (*Aira praecox*) and marram (*Ammophila arenaria*).

Graylings live in discrete colonies, usually containing a few tens or hundreds of adults, although vast populations occur on some heaths and dunes. Most of their lives are spent settled in sunny pockets of bare ground, with the wings tightly closed, leaning edge on to the sun, making them extraordinarily difficult to spot. They cast a shadow only in weak light, when they warm up by sitting sideways to the sun's rays. When disturbed, they fly rapidly in a looping flight for a few metres before floating down into another sunspot.

Distribution and status

Although always a local butterfly, the Grayling was once well distributed in poor arid grassland throughout the British Isles. Most inland colonies have disappeared due to agricultural improvements, reclamation and changed land use, and, in the 1950s–90s, due to the dense swards that developed on rough hillsides in the absence of rabbits.

Today, the Grayling has almost disappeared on chalk and limestone downs, where it is largely confined to abandoned quarries and mines. Although still declining, it remains locally common on heaths in south Wales and England, notably in Dorset, Hampshire and the Breck. Otherwise it is largely confined to the coast, where it is locally abundant and well distributed on rocky cliffs, undercliffs, rough arid grassland, and dune systems everywhere except in north-east England and north Scotland. It breeds on most Western Isles, including the Hebrides, but is absent from the Orkneys and Shetland.

 confirmed range

GATEKEEPER or HEDGE BROWN *Pyronia tithonus*

Adult identification

Average wingspan 40 mm (♂) to 47 mm (♀)

This medium-sized butterfly looks more golden in flight than any Brown except the Wall (page 146), but it is less bright than a Comma or Brown Hair-streak. Seen close-up it is easy to identify, although beginners can confuse it with the larger Meadow Brown (page 158).

▲ *The Gatekeeper differs from the Meadow Brown in having white, not black, dots on the hindwing.*

The Gatekeeper's upperwings have broad grey-brown borders enclosing large orange patches, which are especially bright in the smaller males. Males also have a conspicuous dark scent band across the orange on each forewing. Both sexes have a large black eyespot, usually containing two white pupils, near the tip of the forewings, whereas the Meadow Brown's eye has a single pupil, except in Scotland far beyond the Gatekeeper's range. The Gatekeeper also has one, sometimes several, small white dots on the upper hindwing. The undersides are bright mottled brown on the hindwing and dull orange on the forewing, which again bears a diagnostic eye with twin pupils. Note that any dots on the under hindwings are white, whereas those on the Meadow Brown are black.

Young stages

The **egg** is pale with orange blotches, and is laid singly on grass or nearby vegetation sheltered beneath shrubs. It is almost spherical with 16 or 17 ridges

	Jan	Feb	Mar	Apr	May	Jun	Jul	Aug	Sep	Oct	Nov	Dec
egg												
caterpillar												
chrysalis												
adult												

running from top to bottom, and is hard to find (although readily obtained in captivity.

The **caterpillar** hibernates while small, and is easy to find on appropriate grasses in May; search by torchlight at night when they climb to feed on tender grass blades. When fully grown it is either fawn-coloured or grey with a green tinge, and has dark lines and short white hairs, rather like a Scotch Argus (page 150) or Ringlet (page 164), which has pinker stripes along its flanks.

The **chrysalis** is cream with irregular dark streaks, and is very hard to find. It hangs below grass.

Habitat and behaviour

The Gatekeeper's alternative name, Hedge Brown, is apt for shrubs are invari-ably present wherever this butterfly is found. The caterpillars feed on fine and medium-leaved wild grasses, including bents (*Agrostis* spp.), fescues (*Festuca* spp.), meadow grasses (*Poa* spp.) and couch (*Agropyron repens*): they prefer mid-sized to tallish plants growing in warm spots on the sunny sheltered side of a shrub. Colonies of Gatekeeper can be supported by thin strips of suitable land. Typical sites include hedgerows, warm lanes, rough grassy areas contain-ing scrub and, especially, the edges, rides and glades of sunny woods.

Gatekeepers live in discrete colonies which sometimes contain thousands of individuals. It has a jerky flight and seems to hop in the air, moving between flowers, over shrubs or high among trees. Unlike most Browns, it seldom flies over open grassland or settles on the ground. Despite bramble being a favourite, it has a penchant for yellow flowers, and may be seen in scores jostling for nectar on fleabane or ragwort.

Distribution and status

The Gatekeeper is common in southern English counties and lowland Wales, wherever wild grasses and shrubs grow together. There have been many losses in the flatter landscapes due to the increased shadiness of woods, the loss of hedgerows and the general tidying of the countryside, but it is still one of the features of high summer and may be expected in any suitable habitat in the south.

Like several grass-feeders, it has expanded northwards in England, and has become more widespread near its former range edge during recent warm decades. However, it has a clear-cut limit to its range, and is a local to rare species north of the Midlands, where it is increasingly confined to warm scrubby areas near the sea. In Ireland it is virtually confined to the southern and south-east coast, and although often abundant there, does not appear to be spreading north.

▓▓ confirmed
range

MEADOW BROWN *Maniola jurtina*

Adult identification

Average wingspan 50 mm (♂) to 55 mm (♀); larger in the north

This is the commonest large Brown butterfly in Britain. The male's upper-wings are dusky brown with a blurred black patch from the central forewing to the body. In the corner of each forewing is one small white-pupilled black eye-spot, usually surrounded by a circle of

▲ *A female Meadow Brown basking in weak sunlight with her wings wide open. This is the butterfly most commonly seen in the countryside.*

dull orange. There may also be a faint orange patch below this. This orange patch and the eyespot are much larger and obvious on the female. The Meadow Brown often sits with its wings closed, and the lower hindwing may be all that is visible. This is grey-brown with a slight orange sheen and a zigzag boundary that divides a darker inner half from a brighter outer half. There may be one or several small black dots in the outer half.

This butterfly varies somewhat through-out Britain. It is larger and brighter in the north, where the female's eyespots frequently contain two white pupils, like the Gatekeeper. Both sexes become faded when old. Depending on their age, several Browns look rather like the Meadow Brown in flight, but none should be confused when seen at rest. Note the lack of eyespots on the upper hindwing, and see accounts of Ringlet (page 164) and Gatekeeper (page 156).

Young stages

The **egg** is laid singly on grass, dead veg-etation, or simply dropped to the ground

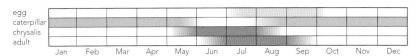

	Jan	Feb	Mar	Apr	May	Jun	Jul	Aug	Sep	Oct	Nov	Dec
egg												
caterpillar												
chrysalis												
adult												

by perched females. It is small (0.5 mm tall), almost spherical with 20–24 ribs from top to bottom, and is pale with orange blotches. It is hard to find but easily obtained in captivity.

The **caterpillar** hibernates when small. It is simple to find by torchlight on spring nights when it climbs grass blades to feed. When fully grown the body is bright green with a dark green stripe down its back and a pale stripe along each side. The tails are white and the body is covered with white hairs, longer than those on the green caterpillars of other Browns.

The **chrysalis** is green with striking broad black stripes on the wing cases. It hangs beneath a grass stem or vegetation and is hard to find.

Habitat and behaviour

The Meadow Brown may be seen in almost any habitat where wild grasses survive. Several native species are eaten by the caterpillar, but those, such as smooth meadow grass (*Poa pratensis*), that have medium-sized rather than very fine or coarse blades are preferred. High densities of this butterfly develop in sunny sheltered spots where the sward is left to grow quite tall and lush, whereas it may be absent or in low numbers where the grass is either cropped short or has become dominated by dense tussocks of coarse species. Small strips of suitable grassland will support a colony, and typical sites include road verges, hedgerows and banks, wasteland, cliffs and undercliffs, the edges, glades and rides of sunny woods, and tallish unfertilized grassland, hay meadows and downs everywhere.

The adults fly in distinct colonies which generally have clear-cut boundaries and which vary in size from a very few individuals to tens of thousands, depending on the habitat. In weak light, they bask with their wings wide open, but in both dull weather and full sunshine the wings are usually closed. Flight is weak, fluttering, and jerky, just above the grassheads as they move from flower to flower.

Distribution and status

The Meadow Brown is probably the commonest butterfly in the countryside of England, Wales, Ireland and Scotland, but is less often seen in gardens and towns since it seldom flies far from its breeding sites. Although countless colonies have been destroyed by agricultural improvements, especially in lowland Britain, it is still to be expected in any wild grassy habitat, except on northern mountains where it is rarely seen at altitudes above 250 m. It is present on most islands, whether large or small, but is absent from the Shetlands. In Orkney, at the limit of its range, it is local and confined to warm south-facing slopes. It is likewise rather local on the north Scottish mainland.

■■■ *confirmed range*

SMALL HEATH *Coenonympha pamphilus*

Adult identification
Average wingspan 34 mm (♂) to 38 mm (♀); 18 mm closed

This is Britain and Ireland's only small

▲ *The Small Heath always settles with its wings closed, but is conspicuous only so long as the forewing is held aloft, as when the weather is good.*

light brown butterfly; female Blues are very much darker, Skippers more golden, and other Browns are considerably larger. The Small Heath always settles with the wings closed, so only the undersides are seen. The under hindwing is pale grey-brown, with slightly darker patches (but no real pattern) near the body, a blurred white mark halfway out, and faint white dots near the outer edge. The forewing is tucked down in bad weather, but usually protrudes as an orange triangle with grey edges and a conspicuous white-pupilled black eyespot near the top corner. The upperwings are tawny, making the whole butterfly light brown when flying. Only the (much larger) north Scottish race of the Large Heath is similar (page 44).

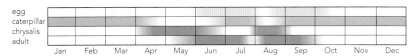

	Jan	Feb	Mar	Apr	May	Jun	Jul	Aug	Sep	Oct	Nov	Dec
egg												
caterpillar												
chrysalis												
adult												

Young stages

The **egg** is bowl-shaped with about 50 thin vertical ridges. Pale yellow, with large rust-coloured blotches, it is laid singly and low down on fine grass blades, making it difficult to find.

The **caterpillar**, though, is encountered quite often, feeding by day on small grass clumps. When fully grown the body is green, with dark white stripes and pink and white pointed tails.

The **chrysalis** is also well camouflaged, but is occasionally found hanging beneath a grass stem; pretty chocolate stripes break up the pale green ground colour.

Habitat and behaviour

The Small Heath is found almost anywhere in Britain where wild fine-leaved grasses survive. The exact range of grasses eaten by the caterpillar is unknown, but fescues (*Festuca* spp.), bents (*Agrostis* spp.) and meadow grasses (*Poa* spp.) are favourites. Most colonies are small, breeding along road verges, hedgerows, sunny woodland rides and in any unimproved grassland. On heavy ground, local dry spots are used, such as boundary banks and ant hills. Better sites occur on well-drained soils, especially where the sward is sparse, fairly (but not very) short, and dominated by fine grasses. Enormous populations can develop in extensive areas of this habitat, for example on dunes, heaths, moorland, the coast, and ancient chalk and limstone downs. Elsewhere, it is normally seen in ones or twos.

In southern Britain, adults can be seen from mid-May to October, as shown in the life-cycle chart. The sequence of broods is complicated because some caterpillars develop much more quickly than others. Farther north, there is probably only one emergence of adults each year, starting in early June in central Scotland but not until July in the far north.

The adults live in close-knit colonies. Long periods are spent at rest, perched in bare spots and leaning with wings closed towards the sun. Flight, when it occurs, is quite rapid, bobbing and weaving just above the grassheads.

Distribution and status

This is one of the most widely distributed butterflies throughout Britain, although it is slightly more local in Ireland. Colonies may be found on mountains as high as 750 m and on almost all offshore islands, however small, except the Shetlands and Orkney. It remains common on well-drained natural habitats throughout its range, although numerous colonies have been eliminated from most lowland grassland in recent years. Despite this, the butterfly can still be expected in ones or twos along banks and road verges except in the most intensively farmed regions.

▓▓ confirmed range

LARGE HEATH *Coenonympha tullia*

Adult identification

Average wingspan 41 mm; about 22 mm closed but larger in northern Scotland

The Large Heath is a grey-brown medium-sized butterfly that never basks with its wings open, so only the under-wings are seen. The sexes are similar, although females may be lighter, with much individual variation in size, colour and spotting within any colony although

▲ *The heavily spotted* davus *form of the Large Heath occurs near the south of its range, as shown here in Shropshire. It is the most distinctive of the three forms.*

the predominant type varies across its range. For simplicity, these are classified into three forms, although every inter-mediate exists, sometimes in the same population:

1) *davus* (pages 19, 44 and above) is the most distinctive and the predominant form in the south. The underwings are dark green-grey with a pale zigzag band running down both wings and a string of eyespots near the outer edge, typically six on the hindwing and two to four on the forewing. The spots are large and black, with white pupils and yellow haloes.

2) *polydama* is paler and larger than *davus*, with the six eyespots on the hind-wing small, rather faint and sometimes lacking white pupils. There are generally one or two similarly reduced eyespots on the forewing.

3) *scotica* (page 44) is the most northern and largest form of the butterfly, and the opposite extreme in markings to *davus*, being pale, grey and blurred, with few or even no tiny faint eyespots which lack a white pupil.

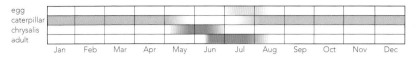

	Jan	Feb	Mar	Apr	May	Jun	Jul	Aug	Sep	Oct	Nov	Dec
egg												
caterpillar												
chrysalis												
adult												

In flight, the grey-brown upperwings are revealed, and the whole butterfly appears grey, with little or no trace of the orange.

Young stages

The **egg** is large for the butterfly's size (0.8 mm high), round with a flattened top, and has about 50 fine ridges running from top to bottom. It is pale, acquiring brown patches as it develops, and is laid singly on the caterpillar's food grasses.

The **caterpillar** hibernates when small. It often feeds by day when older, eating grass blades from the tip downwards. When fully grown it is 25 mm long, grass-green with tiny white hairs and pink and white 'tails', and is striped by dark green down the back and white along the sides. No other Brown has so slender a caterpillar nor one with so large a head.

The **chrysalis** is bright green with dark stripes on the wing case, much like a large Small Heath's. It is formed hanging beneath any dense vegetation.

Habitat and behaviour

The Large Heath lives in boggy places in the north, where the ground is water-logged, often submerged, and some-times treacherous. The caterpillars feed on hare's-tail cottongrass (*Eriophorum vaginatum*) and, less often, cotton grass (*Eriophorum angustifolium*), purple moor grass (*Molinia caerulea*) and sedges. Whatever the foodplant, colonies breed in discrete self-contained areas, and may support up to a few thousand adults. Most are confined to damp moors, peat mosses, and raised blanket bogs, and may be encountered from sea level up to altitudes of 800 m. In Ireland, search especially where small-scale peat digging has created damp hollows within bogs.

Distribution and status

Colonies of Large Heath may be found throughout Ireland, in central and north Wales, and in the northern half of England, but they are uncommon and local in all these countries. Numerous extinctions have occurred, particularly in England, due to the reclamation of bog.

In Scotland, it was always much commoner and has survived a good deal better. It is widely distributed through most of the lowlands and highlands, but is very much more localized in the south. It becomes progressively more common as one travels farther north, and is also found on most isles, including many that are small and most of the Inner and Outer Hebrides. The northern limit is Orkney.

On the map, boundaries have been drawn where the forms *davus*, *polydama* and *scotica* predominate. Note that these divisions are very crude and that many exceptions and intermediates will be found both within colonies and on neighbouring sites.

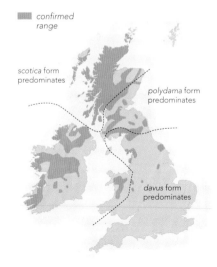

■■■ confirmed range

scotica form predominates

polydama form predominates

davus form predominates

Adult identification
Average wingspan 48 mm (♂) to 52 mm (♀)

This medium-sized butterfly has dark velvety-brown upperwings that are almost black on the male and only slightly lighter on the female (page 45). A fine white fringe runs round the outer edges, making

▲ *The Ringlet is one of the few butterflies that will fly in really overcast weather, and may even be active during light showers.*

a sharp contrast, and there are usually two inconspicuous little black eyespots near the centre of each wing. When settled, the wings are usually closed, revealing the Ringlet's most distinctive feature – a string of conspicuous eyes with white centres surrounded by black then yellow rings. There are generally five to each hindwing with at least two on the forewings, and they gleam conspicuously against a dark, slightly bronzed background.

At rest, the underwings of this butterfly are unmistakable, but old specimens with the wings open look a little like the male Meadow Brown and look very similar when flapping slowly past in flight. Young Ringlets look black when flying.

Young stages
The **eggs** are dropped to the ground among tall wild grasses in damp places, apparently aimlessly by the females. They are impossible to find but can easily be obtained in captivity. Each is globular,

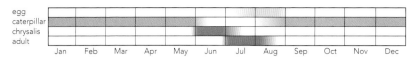

	Jan	Feb	Mar	Apr	May	Jun	Jul	Aug	Sep	Oct	Nov	Dec
egg												
caterpillar												
chrysalis												
adult												

slightly conical, with a straw-coloured glassy sheen.

The **caterpillar** feeds on wild grasses, where it also hibernates when quite small. The following spring it rests upright on a stem, falling into the grass clump in a curled ball if disturbed. It is pale brown when fully grown with a dark stripe down the back and pale pink and white stripes along the sides. It creeps up to feed on the top grass blades after dusk and can be found quite easily by searching knee-high clumps in moist spots by torchlight in early June.

The **chrysalis** is formed within a few strands of silk at the base of a grass clump. It is rounded, pale pinkish-brown with dark streaks and freckles, and is very difficult to find.

Habitat and behaviour

The Ringlet breeds in distinctly damp, but not waterlogged, spots where there are quite tall flushes of native grasses. It is not fully known which species are eaten by the caterpillars, but the range is certainly small – tufted hairgrass (*Deschampsia caespitosa*), couch (*Agropyron repens*) and annual meadow grass (*Poa pratensis*) are favourites. Ringlets live in close-knit colonies that may range in size from a handful of adults up to tens of thousands, depending on the site. Numbers also vary from one year to the next, in general being higher after wet seasons and crashing after a drought.

The largest colonies of this dusky Brown butterfly are found in woodland glades, rides and borders, where the ground vegetation is left to grow tall and lush. Ringlets may occur in moderately shady places, but are rarely found in tall dense conifer plantations. Colonies also breed among scrubby rank grassland and along overgrown hedgerows and verges, especially on heavy soils, but are generally absent from open dry grassland. The adult has a weak fluttering flight and seems almost to hover above the grassheads. It is often seen feeding on brambles, jostling for nectar among Meadow Browns and Skippers.

Distribution and status

The Ringlet is a local but fairly common butterfly in eastern and southern England, Wales, Ireland and increasingly large areas of lowland southern Scotland. It has spread much in the northern half of its range during recent warm years, but is still absent from a large part of north-west England and very few colonies are found in the Scottish Highlands or on isles apart from a few of the Inner Hebrides. In the past, numerous colonies were destroyed by the general tidying up of the countryside, land drainage, and the intensification of agriculture – a process that is causing many losses still in Ireland. Nevertheless, this remains one of our commoner butterflies through most of its range.

▆▆▆ confirmed
range

EXTINCT BUTTERFLIES

In the past 160 years, a number of British butterflies has become extinct, including the Large Copper (last colony 1851), Mazarine Blue (1877), Black-veined White (1922), Large Blue (1979) and Large Tortoiseshell (1980s). The Large Blue has been so successfully re-established in four former regions that it is now included among the main species' accounts (pages 108–109). So too is the Large Tortoiseshell (pages 122–123), which although probably extinct as a breeding species, is still occasionally seen as singletons, partly due to releases of continental specimens and partly due to the odd migrant. Here, a brief description is given of the Large Copper, because it has been regularly introduced to one or two British nature reserves, albeit with little success, and may yet become re-established through the Great Fen Project.

LARGE COPPER *Lycaena dispar*

Wingspan 40 mm (♂), 42 mm (♀)

A beautiful and unmistakable Copper that lived once among the fens of Lincolnshire and Cambridgeshire, breeding along dyke edges and where reeds had been cut. Conspicuous white eggs were laid on the caterpillar's foodplant, great water dock (*Rumex hydrolapathum*). British colonies were of a beautiful subspecies, *dispar*, but this was lost forever when the fens were drained. In one surviving fragment – Wood Walton Fen, Cambridgeshire – the habitat has been restored and a similar Dutch subspecies, *batavus*, was introduced in 1927. Numbers fluctuate greatly, and it had to be reintroduced in 1969, but in good years the adults made an unforgettable sight throughout July. This colony, alas, died out in the 1990s. The linking of Wood Walton with other areas of fenland through the Great Fen project may result in more suitable conditions for this beautiful Copper, and there is some hope that it will be established in the Broads, but at present there is no known colony in Britain.

In addition to Britain's three regular immigrants – the Red Admiral, Painted Lady and Clouded Yellow – a few vagrants reach our shores at irregular intervals, and once or twice a century there is a bumper year when several species arrive, some to breed and become locally common. Unfortunately these temporary inhabitants seldom survive our winters. There is also a growing number of exotic species that escape or are (illegally) released into the British countryside. Foremost among these is the **Geranium Bronze** (*Cacyreus marshalli*), a South African Lycaenid whose caterpillars occasionally arrive among imported pelargonium cultivars. By 2006, the Geranium Bronze had established many wild colonies across southern regions of Europe where garden pelegoniums are winter hardy, but only a handful has been reported in the British Isles. Thus a few adults briefly bred in Sussex in 1997–98, and occasional individuals have been reported from elsewhere since. At the time of writing, it is too rarely sighted to warrant illustration in this guide. Instead, brief accounts are given below of our seven most regular rare immigrants – those that you can hope to encounter at least once in a lifetime.

BATH WHITE *Pontia daplidice*

Although superficially like a female Orange Tip (page 30), the under hindwings are greener and less-fussily patterned, whereas the upperwings have larger, blotchier dark marks. Generally seen in late summer (when rare second-brood Orange Tips also fly) on southern cliffs and downs, it is exceedingly rare, but in 1906 and 1945 appreciable numbers arrived and bred on wild crucifers to produce temporary colonies of tens

and even hundreds of adults in a few south coast localities.

PALE AND BERGER'S CLOUDED YELLOWS
Colias hyale and *C. australis*

These look almost identical and very similar to *helice* Clouded Yellows (see page 32). None can be distinguished in flight, but *helice* always has broader black edges round the hindwings. The ground colour of all is too variable for identification. Note egg-laying plants: Pale Clouded Yellows use trefoils and clovers, and have green caterpillars with yellow stripes; Berger's use horseshoe vetch and their green caterpillars have yellow and black marks. Note, however, that *helice* lays on all these plants.

Pale and Berger's Clouded Yellows immigrate in most years, and naturalists

who frequent southern downs and coasts expect to see one every few years. Berger's is the rarer and *helice* considerably commoner than either. Occasionally large numbers arrive, as in 1900 (2,203 reports) and 1945.

LONG-TAILED BLUE *Lampides boeticus*

This is an attractive active Lycaenid with a rapid jerky flight, more like a fast Hair-streak buzzing round shrubs than any British Blue. When settled, it also resembles some Hairstreaks through its conspicuous tails that wave as it slowly rotates its hindwings, coupled with a reluctance to open its wings. These, however, are easily distinguished from other butterflies due to the brown and fawn mottling, a white band and a distinctive eyespot by the tail. A common species in the southern half of Europe, the Long-tailed Blue occasionally arrives in the British Isles and is generally recorded as singletons, typically two or three times a year along the south English coast or on southern downs. Occasionally it arrives in greater numbers, notably in 1945, and

in any year may form a small second generation through breeding on wild and cultivated legumes. The year 2013 saw another major influx, with sightings, and often breeding, reported in Derbyshire and most southern counties, including along a one-mile stretch of the White Cliffs east of Dover.

CAMBERWELL BEAUTY *Aglais antiopa*

A gorgeous and unmistakable large Nymphalid with dark chocolate-brown upperwings bordered by blue spots and broad cream margins. In contrast to the Monarch, most sightings are in eastern England and Scotland, probably originating from Scandinavia, some perhaps arriving among shipments of timber. However, occasional individuals are reported from all parts of the British Isles, including Ireland. The Camberwell Beauty is seen either in late summer or early spring and seems able to withstand our winters as a hibernating adult, but not, apparently, to breed here, even though its foodplants are willows. Like most

migrants, its appearance is sporadic – a few in most years with occasional large influxes, notably in 1846, 1872, 1976 (272 reports), 1995 (350 sightings) and 2006.

QUEEN OF SPAIN FRITILLARY *Issoria lathonia*

One or two British sightings are made in most years of this medium-sized Fritillary, which may be distinguished from other Fritillaries by very large and numerous silver patches on the under hindwing which positively glint as the butterfly flies rapidly by. Sightings have increased in recent years, notably in Jersey up to the turn of the century, and on the Suffolk coast near Mimsmere in 1995–97, when a temporary breeding colony may have established itself on the wild pansies growing in rough ground and dunes. Another bred briefly in Sussex in 2008–09. Apart from on the coast, immigrants are generally encountered on open downland in south-east England in late spring; very occasionally, these produce a short-lived brood in August.

MONARCH *Danaus plexippus*

This is by far the largest butterfly to be seen in Britain. Nearly twice the size of a Peacock, its unmistakable orange and black wings span 110 mm causing it to flap and glide slowly like a tawny bird. It is an inhabitant of the Canaries and North America, where there are annual migrations covering thousands of kilometres. Adults are occasionally blown off course to Britain, but cannot breed here since the milkweeds that the caterpillars eat are not indigenous. In recent years there have been more-or-less annual sightings of this highly conspicuous butterfly, mainly in the Scillies, Cornwall,

80% life-size

Devon and Dorset notably in 1981, when 140 were reported, 1995 (c. 200 records), 1999 (more than 600 sightings) and 2001 (about 100).

SIX-SPOT BURNET
Zygaena filipendulae

Of the seven species of Burnet moth in Britain, the Six-spot is much the commonest. Its caterpillar feeds on bird's-foot trefoil, and the adult flies from June to August in unfertilized meadows, downs, woodland clearings and along the coast, jostling with butterflies for nectar on flowers.

CINNABAR
Tyria jacobaeae

The gregarious black and yellow hooped caterpillars of this common moth are a familiar sight on ragwort throughout the British Isles. The adult is generally nocturnal, but it frequently makes weak fluttery flights when disturbed by day from May to late July.

SILVER-Y
Autographa gamma

This migrant from Africa and Mediterranean regions arrives in vast numbers every year, to breed on a variety of low-growing plants. It can be seen by day from spring to autumn throughout the British Isles, often in large numbers, in any flower-rich habitat, including gardens.

HUMMING-BIRD HAWK
Macroglossum stellatarum

An increasingly familiar immigrant, seen especially on sunny summer days in the south. It hovers like a hummingbird in front of flowers, drinking nectar through its long proboscis. The caterpillars feed on bedstraw, but the adults are seen in all flower-rich habitats, including gardens.

LATTICED HEATH
Semiothisa clathrata

This small moth is found on moorland, unfertilized grasslands and rough ground throughout Britain, where the caterpillars feed on clovers and lucerne. It generally has two adult generations, flying in May–June and August–September.

BURNET COMPANION
Euclidia glyphica

This is a common day-flying moth in the southern half of Britain, but is scarcer in the north. The caterpillars feed on clovers and trefoils, and the adults fly in summer in open woodland, unfertilized meadows and on downs.

BEAUTIFUL YELLOW UNDERWING *Anarta myrtilli*

A small moth, whose caterpillars feed mainly on heathers. The adults may be seen on heaths and moorland from May to August in the south, and in June and July farther north, flying whenever the sun shines.

CHIMNEY SWEEPER
Odezia atrata

A beautiful day-flying moth that is seen in June and July, especially on chalk and limestone grassland, where the caterpillars feed on pignut.

ORANGE UNDERWING
Archiearis parthenias

A fairly common day-flying moth found in early spring in birch woods in England, Wales and, more locally, Scotland. The caterpillars eat birch catkins and leaves.

EMPEROR
Pavonia pavonia

Only the males of this magnificent moth fly by day, when they search for females in April–May on many British heaths and moorlands. The caterpillar is equally spectacular – green with black hoops and yellow wart-like spots – and may be found by carefully searching heather in summer.

HORNET MOTH
Sesia apiformis

This curious moth is beautifully camouflaged to resemble a hornet. The caterpillars burrow into the wood of poplars in the southern half of Britain, and the adults emerge in June–July.

FURTHER READING AND VIEWING

Asher, J., Warren, M. S., Fox, R., Harding, P., Jeffcoate, G. and Jeffcoate, S. *The Millennium Atlas of Butterflies in Britain and Ireland*, Oxford University Press, 2001. Excellent account of the changing status and natural history of UK butterflies.

Baines, C. *How to Make a Wildlife Garden*, Frances Lincoln, 2000. See page 23.

Barkham, P. *The Butterfly Isles*, Granta Books, 2011. A delightful account of a personal odyssey to see all the British butterflies in one summer.

Salmon, M. *The Aurelian Legacy: British butterflies and their collectors*, Harley Books, Colchester, 2000. A highly enjoyable, well-written and scholarly account of a bygone age. Strongly recommended.

Thomas, Jeremy and Lewington, R. *The Butterflies of Britain and Ireland*, British Wildlife Publishing, 2010, new edition 2014. This prize-winning textbook gives the most up-to-date and comprehensive account of all British butterflies, and is beautifully illustrated by the world's leading butterfly artist.

Tolman, T. *Field Guide to the Butterflies of Britain and Ireland*, Collins, London, 2004. First-class guide – more comprehensive than Mitchell Beazley.

Vickery, M. *Gardening for Butterflies*, Butterfly Conservation Society, East Lulworth, 1998.

Whalley, P. *The Mitchell Beazley Pocket Guide to Butterflies*, Mitchell Beazley, London, 2000. The essential easy-to-use pocket field guide to Europe.

WEBSITES, VIDEOS AND APPS

www.ukbutterflies.co.uk is the most accessible, informative and an altogether delightful website for all information, news, views and illustrations of British (and European) butterflies.

British Butterflies – an interactive guide. A comprehensive multimedia reference DVD-ROM and app from Birdguides that covers the 61 regular British butterfly species, with 200 high-quality video clips of species and interviews with experts.

Patrick Barkham's Guide to British Butterflies, 2013. An enchanting DVD, packed with interest, and with the same knowledgeable yet neatly light touch as Barkham's *The Butterfly Isles*.

SOCIETIES TO JOIN

Butterfly Conservation (www.butterfly-conservation.org)
Membership of this influential society is essential for anyone interested in the natural history of Britain's butterflies and moths or in contributing to their conservation. As well as centres in England, Wales, Scotland and Northern Ireland, there are active local branches in 32 regions: see website for contact details. Activities range from natural history talks, walks and outings to practical conservation projects at all scales from enhancing gardens to monitoring and managing sites of international importance.

Buglife (www.buglife.org)
Buglife is the core organization in Europe devoted to the conservation of all invertebrates. Join it not only for the wealth of fascinating information you will discover but also because it leads in saving Britain's rarest bugs, slugs, snails, bees, wasps, ants, spiders, beetles and other invertebrates.

The Wildlife Trusts (www.wildlifetrusts.org)
Forty-seven different local Wildlife Trusts cover the whole of the UK, the Isle of Man and Alderney: see website for contact details. With more than 800,000 members and 2,300 nature reserves, they already form the largest UK voluntary organization dedicated to conserving all UK habitats and species. Join and support this invaluable movement, for almost every Trust owns a suite of sites that are of local, national and sometimes international importance for butter-flies. There is also a flourishing junior branch, Wildlife Watch, with 150,000 members.

BUTTERFLIES AND THE LAW

An aim of this guide is to encourage naturalists and school-children to learn about butterflies, in all stages of their life, through field observation, photography and by rearing unprotected species in captivity. However, butterfly collect-ing is no longer encouraged nor is the release of captive-bred adults into new habitats, and some activities are illegal. For full details see www.ukbutterflies.co.uk. In brief, it is currently illegal to catch, possess, kill or disturb the adults, eggs, caterpillars or chrysalises – or knowingly to damage the habitat – of Large Blue, Large Copper, Heath Fritillary, High Brown Fritillary, Marsh Fritillary or Swallowtail. Seven-teen additional species are protected from being sold. In Northern Ireland, the same protection extends to the Dingy Skipper, Brimstone, Holly Blue, Purple Hairstreak and Large Heath.

INDEX

Pages numbers in *italic* indicate illustrations; page numbers in ***bold italic*** indicate species descriptions

Adonis Blue 14, 15, 16, *35*, 94, 96, 100, 101, 102, 103, ***104–105***

Bath White 78, *167*
Beautiful Yellow Underwing *171*
Berger's Clouded Yellow 68, *167*
Black Hairstreak 11, *33*, 86, ***88–89***
Black-veined White 166
Brimstone 8, 11, 32, ***70–71***, 72
Brown Argus 15, 16, *34*, 92, 94, ***96–97***, 98, 99, 100
Brown Hairstreak 11, 20, 21, *33*, ***82–83***, 156
Burnet Companion *170*

'Cabbage' White *see* Large and Small Whites
Camberwell Beauty *168*
Chalkhill Blue 16, *17*, *35*, 94, 96, 101, ***102–103***, 104
Chequered Skipper 11, 19, *29*, ***46–47***, 110
Chimney Sweeper *171*
Cinnabar *170*
Clouded Yellow 8, 10, 14, *32*, ***68–69***, 70, 167
Comma 5, 10, 11, 20, 21, *37*, 122, ***126–127***, 146, 156
Common Blue 9, 11, 18, 21, *35*, 84, 96, 98, ***100–101***, 104, 105, 106, 108
Cryptic Wood White 5, *30*, 64, ***66–67***

Dark Green Fritillary 11, 19, *42*, 133, ***134–135***
Dingy Skipper 11, 17, 24, *29*, ***58–59***, 60, 61, 80, 174
Duke of Burgundy 11, 12, 16, 17, 25, *27*, *29*, *41*, 46, 47, ***110–111***, 138

Emperor *172*
Essex Skipper 11, *29*, 48, ***50–51***, 52, 53

Gatekeeper 11, 13, 18, 20, 21, *44*, 45, 82, 150, 151, ***156–157***, 158
Glanville Fritillary *41*, 138, ***140–141***
Grayling 14, *18*, *44*, ***154–155***

Green Hairstreak 11, 15, 16, 18, 26, *33*, ***80–81***
Green-veined White 11, 20, 21, *30*, 64, 73, 74, ***76–77***, 78
Grizzled Skipper 11, *29*, 58, ***60–61***

Heath Fritillary *40*, ***142–143***, 174
Hedge Brown *see* Gatekeeper
High Brown Fritillary *41*, ***132–133***, 134, 135, 174
Holly Blue 10, 11, 16, 20, 21, 22, 23, 26, *34*, 84, 92, 100, ***106–107***, 108, 174
Hornet Moth *172*
Humming-bird Hawk *170*

Large Blue 4, 5, 14, 15, *34*, 100, ***108–109***, 166, 174
Large Copper 4, *166*, 174
Large Heath *19*, *44*, 160, ***162–163***, 174
Large Skipper 11, 16, 20, *29*, 54, ***56–57***
Large Tortoiseshell 11, *37*, 120, ***122–123***, 166
Large White 23, *31*, 60, 70, ***72–73***, 74, 75, 76
Latticed Heath *170*
Little Blue *see* Small Blue
Long-tailed Blue *168*
Lulworth Skipper *29*, 48, 50, ***52–53***, 54, 56

Marbled White 11, *16*, 26, 27, *43*, ***152–153***
Marsh Fritillary 11, 19, *41*, ***138–139***, 140, 174
Mazarine Blue 166
Meadow Brown 11, 13, 20, *45*, 145, 156, ***158–159***, 164, 165
Monarch 168. *169*
Mountain Ringlet 19, *45*, ***148–149***, 150

Northern Brown Argus 19, *34*, 96, ***98–99***

Orange Tip 11, 20, 21, 23, *30*, 73, 74, ***78–79***, 167
Orange Underwing *172*

Painted Lady 8, 11, 18, 20, 38, ***118–119***, 167
Pale Clouded Yellow 68, *167*
Peacock 10, 11, 13, 20, 21, *23*, *38*, 120, 121, ***124–125***, 127, 169
Pearl-bordered Fritillary 10, *40*, 128, 129, ***130–131***

Purple Emperor *7*, 11, 13, 27, *36*, 112, ***114–115***
Purple Hairstreak 11, *13*, 15, *33*, ***84–85***, 86, 174

Queen of Spain Fritillary *169*

Red Admiral 8, 11, 20, 23, *38*, ***116–117***, 118, 167
Ringlet 11, 45, 145, 157, 158, ***164–165***

Scotch Argus 11, 19, *45*, 148, ***150–151***, 156
Silver-spotted Skipper 14, 15, *29*, 52, ***54–55***, 56
Silver-studded Blue *7*, *15*, 18, *35*, ***94–95***, 100
Silver-washed Fritillary 11, *42*, 132, 134, ***136–137***
Silver-y *170*
Six-spot Burnet *24*, *170*
Small Blue 16, 26, *34*, ***92–93***, 94, 98, 106
Small Copper 11, 16, 17, 18, 21, 26, *33*, ***90–91***, 110
Small Heath 11, 17, 18, *44*, ***160–161***, 163
Small Pearl-bordered Fritillary 11, *40*, ***128–129***, 130
Small Skipper 11, 20, *29*, ***48–49***, 53, 57, 59
Small Tortoiseshell 8, 20, *22*, *37*, ***120–121***, 122
Small White 8, 10, 20, 22, *31*, 73, ***74–75***, 76, 77, 79
Speckled Wood 6, 11, 12, 13, 20, *43*, ***144–145***, 147
Swallowtail 6, 26, *39*, ***62–63***, 174

Wall Brown 11, 27, *43*, 144, ***146–147***
White Admiral 11, 12, 13, 27, *36*, ***112–113***, 114, 145
White-letter Hairstreak 11, 12, *33*, 84, ***86–87***, 174
Wood White 5, 11, 26, *30*, ***64–65***, 66, 67

Aglias antiopa 168
Aglais polychloros 11, *37*, 120, ***122–123***, 166
Aglais urticae 8, 20, *22*, *37*, ***120–121***, 122
Anarta myrtilli 171
Anthocharis cardamines 11, 20, 21, 23, *30*, 73, 74, ***78–79***, 167
Apatura iris 7, 11, 13, 27, *36*, 112, ***114–115***

Aphantopus hyperantus 11, 45, 145, 157, 158, *164–165*
Archiearis parthenias 172
Argynnis adippe 41, *132–133*, 134, 135, 174
Argynnis aglaja 11, 19, 42, 133, *134–135*
Argynnis paphia 11, 42, 132, 134, *136–137*
Aricia agestis 15, 16, *34*, 92, 94, *96–97*, 98, 99, 100
Aricia artaxerxes 19, *34*, 96, *98–99*
Autographa gamma 170

Boloria euphrosyne 10, *40*, 128, 129, *130–131*
Boloria selene 11, *40*, *128–129*, 130

Callophrys rubi 11, 15, 16, 18, 26, *33*, *80–81*
Carterocephalus palaemon 11, 19, 29, *46–47*, 110
Celastrina argiolus 10, 11, 16, 20, 21, 22, 23, 26, *34*, 84, 92, 100, *106–107*, 108, 174
Coenonympha pamphilus 11, 17, 18, 44, *160–161*, 163
Coenonympha tullia 19, 44, 160, *162–163*, 174
Colias australis 68, 167
Colias croceus 8, 10, 14, *32*, *68–69*, 70, 167
Colias hyale 68, 167
Cupido minimus 16, 26, *34*, *92–93*, 94, 98, 106

Danaus plexippus 168, *169*

Erebia aethiops 11, 19, *45*, 148, *150–151*, 156
Erebia epiphron 19, *45*, *148–149*, 150
Erynnis tages 11, 17, 24, *29*, *58–59*, 60, 61, 80, 174
Euclidia glyphica 171
Euphydryas aurinia 11, 19, 41, *138–139*, 140, 174

Gonepteryx rhamni 8, 11, 32, *70–71*, 72

Hamearis lucina 11, 12, 16, 17, 25, 27, 29, *41*, 46, 47, *110–111*, 138
Hesperia comma 14, 15, *29*, 52, *54–55*, 56
Hipparchia semele 14, *18*, 44, *154–155*

Inachis io 10, 11, 13, 20, 21, *23*, *38*, 120, 121, *124–125*, 127, 169
Issoria lathonia 169

Lampides boeticus 168
Lasiommata megera 11, 27, *43*, 144, *146–147*
Leptidea juvernica 5, *30*, 64, *66–67*
Leptidea sinapis 5, 11, 26, *30*, *64–65*, 66, 67
Limenitis camilla 11, 12, 13, 27, *36*, *112–113*, 114, 145
Lycaena dispar 4, *166*, 174
Lycaena phlaeas 11, 16, 17, 18, 21, 26, *33*, *90–91*, 110

Macroglossum stellatarum 170
Maculinea arion 4, 5, 14, 15, *34*, 100, *108–109*, 166, 174
Maniola jurtina 11, 13, 20, *45*, 145, 156, *158–159*, 164, 165
Melanargia galathea 11, *16*, 26, 27, *43*, *152–153*
Melitaea athalia 40, *142–143*, 174
Melitaea cinxia 41, 138, *140–141*

Neozephyrus quercus 11, *13*, 15, *33*, *84–85*, 86, 174

Ochlodes venata 11, 16, 20, *29*, 54, *56–57*
Odezia atrata 171

Papilio machaon 6, 26, *39*, *62–63*, 174
Pararge aegeria 6, 11, 12, 13, 20, 43, *144–145*, 147
Pavonia pavonia 172
Pieris brassicae 23, *31*, 60, 70, *72–73*, 74, 75, 76
Pieris napi 11, 20, 21, *30*, 64, 73, 74, *76–77*, 78
Pieris rapae 8, 10, 20, 22, *31*, 73, *74–75*, 76, 77, 79
Plebejus argus 7, *15*, 18, *35*, *94–95*, 100
Polygonia c-album 5, 10, 11, 20, 21, *37*, 122, *126–127*, 146, 156
Polyommatus bellargus 14, 15, 16, *35*, 94, 96, 100, 101, 102, 103, *104–105*
Polyommatus coridon 16, 17, *35*, 94, 96, 101, *102–103*, 104

Polyommatus icarus 9, 11, 18, 21, *35*, 84, 96, 98, *100–101*, 104, 105, 106, 108
Pontia daplidice 78, *167*
Pyrgus malvae 11, *29*, 58, *60–61*
Pyronia tithonus 11, 13, 18, 20, 21, *44*, 45, 82, 150, 151, *156–157*, 158

Satyrium pruni 11, *33*, 86, *88–89*
Satyrium w-album 11, 12, *33*, 84, *86–87*, 88
Semiothisa clathrata 171
Sesia apiformis 172

Thecla betulae 11, 20, 21, *33*, *82–83*, 156
Thymelicus acteon *29*, 48, 50, *52–53*, 54, 56
Thymelicus lineola 11, *29*, 48, *50–51*, 52, 53
Thymelicus sylvestris 11, 20, *29*, *48–49*, 53, 57, 59
Tyria jacobaeae 170

Vanessa atalanta 8, 11, 20, 23, *38*, *116–117*, 118, 167
Vanessa cardui 8, 11, 18, 20, *38*, *118–119*, 167

Zygaena filipendulae 24, *170*

PHOTOGRAPHIC ACKNOWLEDGEMENTS

Margaret Brooks 64; Tom Brereton 17, 60; D. W. H. Clark 50, 52, 54, 56, 58, 62, 70, 80, 84, 88, 90, 96, 102, 110, 116, 118, 120, 124, 134, 152, 156, 158; Jeremy Thomas 4, 7, 9, 12, 13, 14, 15, 16, 21, 24, 100, 108, 114; Robert Thompson 22/23, 66, 78, 140; Ken Willmott 17, 18, 19, 46, 48, 68, 72, 74, 76, 82, 86, 92, 94, 104, 106, 112, 122, 126, 128, 130, 132, 136, 138, 142, 144, 146, 148, 150, 154, 160, 162, 164.

All butterfly and moth illustrations: Richard Lewington.

Life-cycle illustrations: Ken Oliver with additional coloration by Pete Mallinson.